A Gentleman of Glamorgan:

Iolo Morganwg, the Prince of Wales, and the Gentry of Glamorgan

Emlyn Phillips MSc MBA

First published 2023
by Rowanvale Books Ltd
The Gate
Keppoch Street
Roath
Cardiff
CF24 3JW
www.rowanvalebooks.com

A CIP catalogue record for this book is available from the British Library.
ISBN: 978-1-914422-41-6

To the memory of my parents, June and Graham Phillips, who contributed so much to the community of Cowbridge.

Table of Contents

Acknowledgements 7

Introduction...9

1. Iolo's Glamorgan 15

2. Mary Nicholl of Remenham.................................25

3. Edward Mathew 30

4. The Edwins 42

5. Ann Matthew's Mother and Aunt 48

6. The Nicholls..60

7. A Bardic Introduction in Llanmaes: John
Bradford 71

8. The Prince of Wales...75

9. Mary Robinson 79

10. Williams, Walters, and Malkin 95

11. Kitty Deere and Margaret Roberts 104

12. Llywellyn Traherne and Daniel Jones 115

13. A Mother's Aspirations 119

14. Iolo Morganwg as a Member of the Gentry...........124

References 130

Index..153

Author Profile...164

Acknowledgements

Many thanks to Dr Robin Darwall-Smith, who generously provided information on John Nicholl of Remenham's Oxford career.

The cover photograph of the stained-glass window from Cowbridge Grammar School, now in Holy Cross Church, is used with the kind permission of the rector and church wardens of Holy Cross Parish Church, Cowbridge, August 2022.

Introduction

On 8 April 1795, George Frederick Augustus of the House of Hanover, Prince of Wales, married his cousin, Princess Caroline of Brunswick. At the time of their engagement the previous year, they had never met. The prince had been forced to agree to it by his father, King George III, in exchange for the king paying off some of the prince's debts. These were enormous: the prince lived a dissipated life of drinking and gambling and had multiple mistresses.

As part of the wedding celebrations, an obscure Welsh stonemason arrived at Carlton House, the prince's sumptuous home in the heart of London. He was there to deliver a poem he had written in praise of the marriage, dedicated to the prince. In eighteenth-century society, such a dedication required prior permission, which the prince had granted.

This was not their first interaction. In January of the previous year, the stonemason, Edward Williams of Glamorgan, had, after years of effort, published a critically well-received two-volume collection of his poetry, similarly dedicated with permission to the Prince of Wales.

In such cases, it was customary for the author to receive a generous gratuity for their work from the person to whom it was dedicated. The Prince of Wales was liberal with his money, and Williams expected to be well-rewarded. That day, he had dressed himself deliberately in his working outfit of leather apron and tool bag, and as he entered Carlton House, his expectations were high indeed.

Those expectations were to be crushed. He was dismissed with a tiny, almost insulting, sum of money, a fraction of what he had anticipated. His hopes shattered, he had no alternative but to leave London for good, walking home to the wife and children waiting for him in Wales, whom he would now be unable to raise out of poverty. There, his works would bring him no prosperity, but they would establish him in the pantheon of Welsh cultural heroes, under his bardic *nom de plume*: Iolo Morganwg.

The purpose of this monograph is to examine how Iolo came to be in Carlton House on that day, and why the prince was so unexpectedly ungenerous. In doing so, it will not focus on Iolo himself, but more on the network of family and social connections and relationships of which he was a part – and, in particular, his place amongst the gentry of Glamorgan.

History is always an interpretation, to a greater or lesser extent. Original materials and later documentation are sorted and assessed, and then interpreted. The product will inevitably be influenced by the prejudices and assumptions of the historian, depending on how aware he or she is of them, and our understanding of Iolo Morganwg is no exception.

Iolo was a fascinating and complex personality: an outstanding poet, a talented stonemason, an intellectual, a political radical, a religious organiser, an antiquarian and early archaeologist, an agricultural improver... The list of his talents is very long indeed. Through his institution of the Gorsedd of the Bards of the Island of Britain, the national myth of Welsh history which he developed, and his vision of a Wales which possessed institutions such as a national academy, a national library, and a national university, he inspired following generations to resist the Anglicisation policies of the nineteenth-century British Empire and to begin the creation of a modern Wales able to proudly take its place amongst the small nations of the world.

Given Iolo's long life and his wealth of talent across a wide range of fields, it is easy to find material to justify a particular narrative about him. Past biographers have perhaps been too keen to fit Iolo into one narrative: the working-class, impoverished "mason-poet" persona he adopted to market himself to the gentry and aristocracy of England, and to the Prince of Wales. Additionally, as the "Bard of Liberty", Iolo has been squeezed into another narrative, that of a democratic pioneer and early exemplar of a form of liberal ideals particularly appealing to his biographers of the twentieth and early twenty-first centuries.

This has, I believe, led most of these biographers to avoid asking questions and to downplay facts which might present a rather different picture: one probably closer to the way that Iolo actually saw himself. Based on the available evidence, it is much more likely that Iolo considered himself to be a member of the gentry class – and that the gentry of Glamorgan felt the same.

In this book, I will justify this suggestion on the basis of documents which have not been discussed by previous biographers and by re-evaluating some of those which have. There are a number of questions which should have been asked before but have not been. My approach is to view Iolo not as a discrete individual, but as a member of a social network whose members interacted with each other as well as with Iolo. This is not intended to be a general biography: the reader will benefit greatly from already being familiar with the different stages of Iolo's life and with the various activities and ventures upon which he tried to improve his family's position.

Since one aim of this text is to establish Iolo Morganwg as a member of the gentry, it will be useful to clarify what the term means. Howell (1986, pp.7–8) provides a useful working definition: the gentry were the class which did not have to work for a living, but who were not aristocrats. They might have had minor titles (esquire, knight, baronet) or they may have simply been known as a "gentleman". In almost all cases, their freedom from work was derived from the ownership of land, which might be farmed on their behalf by an estate manager or leased to tenant farmers. As we will see, being a member of the gentry was not necessarily a matter of birth; commoners could, and frequently did, join their ranks through succeeding in a profession or business and then acquiring an estate, either through purchase or marriage. The size of an estate could vary wildly; leading members might own very large amounts of land, while minor gentry might own barely enough to justify their status as a "gentleman".

Aristocrats, in contrast, were largely members of a hereditary class, holding one or more titles originally conferred by the sovereign, and their estates tended to be much larger. A significant difference is that the gentry tended to live on their own estates, whereas aristocrats tended to be absentee owners, spending most of their time in London or other main cities of the time.

As an aside, it is worth mentioning here that during the eighteenth century, the spelling of names had not yet been standardised, and so they often appear in different forms in different sources; this variety is reflected in this text.

This narrative takes as its starting point 1791: the year Iolo Morganwg began his quest to achieve literary success in English. Publishing a collection of his work was something that had been on his mind for many years, but this was the year he began his attempt in earnest.

To publish his poems – Volumes I and II of *Poems, Lyrical and Pastoral* – he first needed to win the financial backing of subscribers and booksellers. The gentry of Glamorgan were early supporters, but there were not enough of them; he needed to find others amongst the gentry and aristocracy of England and beyond. To increase his potential financial rewards, he also needed to be able to dedicate his work to a wealthy patron.

His key ally in achieving these goals was to be Mrs Mary Nicholl, the wife of the Reverend John Nicholl, rector of the parish of Remenham in Berkshire. She gave him introductions to powerful and wealthy people in London, coached him on how to deal with them, and made sure that he followed up on his meetings with them in order to keep their support. It has also been assumed that it was Mary Nicholl who managed to win him permission to dedicate his work to one of the most important people in the country: the Prince of Wales (Jenkins, 2009, p.32). However, her help was short-lived; by the end of the same year, Mary Nicholl and Iolo had had a bitter falling-out.

Who was Mary Nicholl, and what was her connection to Iolo Morganwg? Our answer needs to begin in the county whose name Iolo had adopted and which he would champion throughout his life and works: Glamorgan.

1. Iolo's Glamorgan

On 25 January 2008, the workers at Tower Colliery, in Glamorgan's Cynon Valley, worked their final shifts and went home. The pit, whose name dates to 1864, had finally run out of coal (*The Independent*, 2008). With Tower's closure, the age of coal in Glamorgan came to an end.

The coal industry, its mining communities, and their working-class culture and politics had dominated the economy of Glamorgan for over a century. They dominated the popular perception of Glamorgan for much longer, and, to an extent, still do. To many people, Glamorgan was the coal industry (and, to a lesser extent, steel), and the coal industry of Glamorgan meant the upland hills and valleys. Without coal and steel, what is Glamorgan other than a name?

As the traces and memories of coal mining fade away into history, they join an earlier Glamorgan – the much older and, in many ways, more Welsh Glamorgan which existed for centuries before the industrial revolution and which was displaced by the growth of heavy industry, and the accompanying vast population growth, during the nineteenth century.

Iolo Morganwg saw the beginnings of this transformation. His work and vision shaped the new Welsh-speaking culture which emerged in response to the economic and demographic changes of the industrial revolution. However, he was the product of an earlier Glamorgan: one which perhaps needs to be remembered and celebrated as relevant to the Glamorgan of the twenty-first century. His story connects the contemporary county to what it was before the coal industry came to dominate.

What was Glamorgan like in the year 1791?

Geographically, Glamorgan is divided into two distinct parts. The hilly uplands, or *blaenau*, sweep down from the mountains of Brecon and mid Wales before abruptly dropping away to the fertile lowlands of the Vale: *y Fro*.

Historically, the Welsh lordship of Glamorgan was derived from the kingdom of Glywysing, which was often at war with both the Welsh princes of north and south-west Wales and with the Saxons of Mercia. Caught between the two, the princes of what became "Morgan's land" decided to submit to the power of Wessex, and so remained outside the sphere of the Welsh dynasties of the north. The territory ruled by the Lords of Glamorgan seems to have varied: at times, they appear to have held territory west of the Tywi, in what is now Carmarthenshire, while for long periods they also ruled over most of what is now Gwent (Smith, 1971, pp.2–5).

Welsh rule of Glamorgan finally came to an end during the rule of William the Conqueror's son, William Rufus. The Norman conquest of Saxon England was more or less complete, but there was still a hunger for new lands, and the Welsh princes could be troublesome neighbours. According to popular history, Robert Fitzhamon, Baron of Gloucester, seized the lordship from Iestyn ap Gwrgant after being invited to intervene in a feud between the local Welsh nobility. Fitzhamon's possessions in England – which included large tracts of lands in Somerset (including Bristol) and Devon (Evans, 1943, p.66) as well as Gloucestershire – were a part of the feudal system introduced by the Normans. In return for his lands, he owed fealty to the King of England. He held Morgannwg, however, through his own efforts and here he was sovereign, answerable to nobody but himself. His heirs and successors, raised to the status of Earls of Gloucester, continued this dual status: subject to the king in Gloucester, but sovereign Marcher lord in Glamorgan.

There was a trade-off for this. To maintain his independence from the English crown, Fitzhamon had to depend on his own forces to rule Glamorgan. Traditionally, these were twelve knights and a few thousand footmen. These had been able to overcome the Welsh forces in battle, but they would not be sufficient to put down a sustained resistance; Glamorgan was, after all, the home of the famed and much-feared Welsh longbow, which could pierce the Normans' armour. Fitzhamon was by necessity forced to be magnanimous to the defeated Welsh.

His own supporters were granted lands in the rich lowland Vale, where they built castles and established manors according to the Norman system, which they ruled according to Norman, and later English, law when dealing with their new English tenants. With their Welsh tenants, however, Welsh law and customs were followed. The nature of the community was often reflected in place names, such as the difference between St Donats (on the coast of the Vale, where English was spoken and English law followed) and Welsh St Donats (in the uplands, where the language and law were Welsh). In the upland *blaenau* the local Welsh aristocratic families were largely permitted to keep their lands in return for swearing fealty to Fitzhamon, and also continued to rule according to Welsh law and custom, including the terms of inheritance set out in the Laws of Hywel Dda. Some of Iestyn ap Gwrgant's sons were also granted lands, in order to bind them to the new ruler. However, two parishes of upland territory were taken for Fitzhamon's own use as hunting grounds, and these became known as *Tir Iarll* – the Earl's Land (Jones, 1955, p.111).

The relationship between Norman and Welsh remained uneasy, and there were regular rebellions. Over time, though, some of these Norman families, particularly the Turbervilles of Coity, integrated so much into the native culture that they had become Welsh in every respect, including their language (Lewis, 1971, p.307), as did the Aubreys, the Herberts, and the Stradlings (Jones, 1976, p.31). The Turbervilles and the St Quintins of Talyfan were considered to have acquired status within the Welsh nobility as well as Norman, and thus formed part of the Lordship of Glamorgan, which remained under Welsh rule (Smith, 1971, p.23). The native Welsh nobility remained a powerful and enduring influence until the late thirteenth century, when the de Clare family, now in possession of Gloucester and Glamorgan, finally exerted control over them (Altschul, 1971, p.57). Nevertheless, both the Welsh of Glamorgan and their Norman overlords were wary of interference from the monarch in London, and this common enemy drew them together (Bryant, 1912, p.41). This led to a strong military connection; it was men of Glamorgan who saved Edward, the Black Prince, when he was thrown from his horse at the Battle of Crécy, for example (ibid., p.42).

This Cambro-Norman entity lived alongside the independent Welsh dynasties of Gwynedd and Deheubarth for over a century. When Edward I finally snuffed out the independent Welsh princes and took their lands, he imposed discriminatory policies on the native population. However, he only ruled the counties of Anglesey, Caernarfon, Meirionydd, Cardigan, and Carmarthen, where he imposed English law (Ogwen Williams, 1960, p.16). None of this applied in Glamorgan, where Welsh law remained in force (in cases where everyone concerned was Welsh, or between a landowner and Welsh tenants), and Welshman and Englishman had equal status in legal disputes (Williams, 1919, p.41). This was because the king's writ did not run in Glamorgan; it was an independent entity, where he had very little authority (Evans, 1943, p.67; Altschul, 1971, p.67). Henry VIII, for example, became the Lord of Glamorgan in his youth, having inherited the title from his great-uncle, Jasper Tudor. When he became king, he was referred to as "King of England and Lord of Glamorgan" (Evans, 1943, p.93). In the centuries before the Welshman Henry Tudor became king, therefore, the Welsh of Glamorgan had had quite a different experience from that of the Welsh of the north and west.

At the time of Henry VIII, there were an astonishing one hundred and forty-one sovereign Marcher lordships, none of which were subject to Henry's authority as king (ibid.; Morris, 1907, pp.317–8). Henry's Acts of Union, which abolished the Marcher lordships and created counties on the English model two hundred years before Iolo Morganwg was born, created a new Wales. Before then, the Welsh had been subjected to the rule of either Marcher lords who answered to no one but themselves or had been in areas nominally subject to the Crown, but which in reality were almost forgotten: a power vacuum where the law was distant. Cattle-rustling, vendettas, and banditry were the everyday norm and were rarely punished, as criminals crossed from one domain to another (Pugh, 1971, pp.565–6). By instituting the English system of shires, local Justices of the Peace, and a new court system, all subject to a rudimentary form of democracy, Henry brought a new peace and prosperity (Williams, 1919, pp.7– 9).

Not all were happy: the new arrangement brought English law to replace the Laws of Hywel Dda, imposing the same legal system on the Marchers as that which had applied in the Principality of Wales for the previous two and a half centuries (Ogwen Williams, 1960, pp.16–18). The English system of primogeniture replaced the traditional Welsh system of inheritance. Worst of all, the Welsh language lost its legal status, with English becoming the only official language of state and law. Nevertheless, the new system was rapidly accepted, and since the administration of justice was given to the King's Great Sessions in Wales (Monmouthshire excepted), Wales remained a separate entity from England. By Iolo's day, this system was well-entrenched, and most of the gentry, the Justices of the Peace in Wales, and the officials they appointed were still Welsh speakers well into the eighteenth and nineteenth centuries (ibid., p.23). This will be of some significance in Iolo's story.

Following the Norman Conquest, the lowland Vale gradually, but not completely, became English-speaking. Over the centuries, though, the Welsh language regained its dominance, and by the fifteenth century, most of Glamorgan was predominantly Welsh, with many more of the gentry families not only speaking the language but also acting as patrons to its poets (Lewis, 1971, pp. 494–6), whose profession had its stronghold in *Tir Iarll* (ibid., pp.501-509). By Iolo Morganwg's birth, the tide had started to turn back to some extent towards English in the Vale, but the uplands were still solidly Welsh speaking. During his lifetime, though, it turned again towards Welsh, which, by the time of his death, was the preferred language of most of the Glamorgan populace, including the Vale – the most senior social strata excepted (James, 1972, p.24).

The upland *blaenau* of Glamorgan were areas where the economy was based on raising livestock, on dairy products, and on producing clothing (Williams, 1965, p.174). They also sent products such as wool, hides, and some garments to markets in the west of England, with the products dispatched via the ports in the south of the county. Live animals were also moved overland to Somerset by drovers (ibid., pp.175–176). In the lowland Vale, there was more diversity, with large amounts of hay and corn being grown in amounts so great that the harvest required seasonal work gangs from elsewhere in Wales, western England and even Ireland (ibid., pp.178–179).

Glamorgan's access to the sea made trade across the Bristol Channel easy. Furthermore, the fact that the

Lords of Glamorgan had also been the Earls of Gloucester meant that there were many social connections, and it was common for gentry and aristocratic families to own land in Somerset or Devon as well as Glamorgan. With the growth of Bristol serving the growing British Empire and the slave trade, Glamorgan became further integrated into a booming global economy, to a far greater extent than other parts of Wales. Glamorgan was prosperous.

As the eighteenth century progressed, so did industrialisation. The tin plate industry had been established at Pontypool in 1720 (Twiston Davies & Edwards, 1939, p.101). The Dowlais ironworks had been established in 1747 (ibid., p.94). Large-scale coal exploitation had begun at Neath as early as the 1690s (ibid., pp.91-2).

The first canal in Glamorgan ran from Merthyr Tydfil to the sea at Penarth; it was begun in 1790 and completed in 1794. Another canal was dug between Neath and Aberpergwm from 1791 to 1798 (Twiston Davies & Edwards, 1939, p.30). Roads in Wales were generally very badly maintained, and travel was difficult (ibid., p.27). However, Glamorgan was improving quickly. In 1764, while Iolo was still a teenager, a group of the local gentry obtained an Act of Parliament permitting them to establish a turnpike trust in order to improve the road between Cardiff and Swansea. Five years later, the English agricultural reformer and writer Arthur Young visited Cowbridge and noted that the road was "exceedingly good" (James & Francis, 1979, p.60). The mail was carried in sacks on horseback; the first mail coaches did not appear until 1784 (Twiston Davies & Edwards, 1939, p.33).

For most of Iolo's lifetime, Glamorgan was the second-most populous county in Wales after

Carmarthenshire, slipping into first place only at the very end of the eighteenth century (Thomas, 1976, p.11). The explosive growth of the industrial revolution did not take place until decades after Iolo's death. Society remained much as it had always been, with tenants renting their land from the gentry and being directed by their landlord when it came to religion or politics (ibid., p.14), on pain of being thrown off their land if they did not obey the landlord's wishes (Grant, 1978, pp.13–14).

It was a time of great change, but the gentry network remained strong and deeply rooted in Glamorgan land, life, and society. In Iolo's lifetime, once-humble families were rising to importance while those that had been prominent for centuries were dying out. As we will see, Iolo was connected to both and as such was a bridge between the ancient past and the new world that was emerging.

In 1700, the gentry were still concentrated in the area where Fitzhamon's knights had established their manors, the very south of the Vale. A century later, new country estates had spread to the *blaenau*. A demographic shift was occurring as the male lines of the ancient Glamorgan families died out and the family heiresses married English aristocrats, industrialists, and entrepreneurs. These new men, however, often sought to maintain the identity and status of the families into which they had married and made great efforts to place themselves within an ongoing continuity of the Glamorgan gentry going back into history – even if that continuity needed to be tweaked, or the history invented (Jenkins, 1984). Iolo Morganwg, whose wider family networks were a part of this transformation, found amongst them a willing audience for his historical imaginings; it suited the new gentry very well (ibid., pp.48–49).

The Welsh of Iolo's time were proud of their language and history, but they were losing the ties that had bound them together as a nation. The localism of the gentry families and the difficulties of travel served to keep communities separate and to emphasise the differences between them. In the Gower, for example, communities only a few miles apart kept themselves separate and regarded each other as "thieves and rogues", while the Welsh of one county would regard those of the next as "foreign and unusual" (Twiston Davies & Edwards, 1939, p.20).

Glamorgan was as thoroughly Welsh as any other part of Wales. However, its Marcher history set it apart from the north and west of Wales, who looked back to the days of the independent princes. Its prosperity, its access to the sea, and its historic links to the west of England also meant that it had a different nature from the Welsh 'heartlands' – and this underlies Iolo's lifelong promotion and defence of his home county.

Having established the context of Iolo's home county, we can move on to discuss Mary Nicholl of Remenham.

2. Mary Nicholl of Remenham

Mary Nicholl was born on 12 February 1748, the year after Iolo Morganwg, as the Honourable Mary Flower (Debrett, 1823, p.1131). She was the third child, and second daughter, of Captain Henry Flower, 2nd Baron Castle Durrow; her grandfather had been made a Baron in 1733. The family were Irish Protestants and for several generations had lived in Finglas, on the edge of Dublin. Their main estate, from which they took their title, was at Durrow, then in County Kilkenny. During the period of Cromwell's Commonwealth, one ancestor had been arrested for supporting the exiled Royalist leader, the Marquis of Ormond; another had been outlawed for the same reason (Vicars, 1908, p.195).

Captain Flower was also the 1st Viscount Ashbrook; the title was created for him on 30 September 1751 (Burke & Burke, 1915, p.139), and was an important increase in social rank (Debrett's, n.d.). His date of birth is unclear – it may have been 1720 (Cracroft-Brennan, n.d.) – but he married in 1740 (Burke & Burke,

1915, p.139), and inherited the title of Baron in either 1746 (ibid.) or 1747 (Vicars, 1908, p.196). He served the British crown as the commander of a troop of horses (ibid.), and it may be that this was connected to his elevation in rank, as his dates are compatible with the War of the Austrian Succession (1740–1748). Possibly he participated in the 1743 Battle of Dettingen, in which George II became, at the age of 60, the last British monarch to personally lead his army into battle (Orr, 2001) – and was victorious, continuing to fight on foot after losing his horse (Maynard Bridge, 1922, p.237). Even if Henry Flower had not been at Dettingen, the king would have paid attention to any actions of distinction during the war, since he himself had had a distinguished career as a cavalryman – at the Battle of Oudenarde in 1708, for example, when he was 25, his horse was shot from beneath him (ibid., p.112) as he fought French and Jacobite forces (Maynard Bridge, 1922, pp.214–215).

It is important to note that the Flower family's titles belonged to the Irish peerage, not the English. At the time, although it had been under English rule for centuries, Ireland was still legally a separate kingdom and was not a part of the United Kingdom of England and Scotland. It had its own House of Commons in Dublin – one of Mary's ancestors had been the Speaker of the House – and its own House of Lords. This meant that Irish peers were not entitled to sit in the House of Lords in London and, consequently, their ranks were perceived as somewhat second-rate compared to their equivalents in the English and Scottish peerages. Davenport, for example, describes Lord Lucan, the brother-in-law of Georgiana, Duchess of Devonshire, as "a mere Irish peer", whose family was of no great distinction (1998, p.73). However, the Flowers also owned land in Britain; until 1854 their main residence here was Beaumont Lodge in Old Windsor, Berkshire (Mitford, 1847, p.83; Levi, n.d.), roughly twenty-five miles from Oxford and forty miles from London. For most of the eighteenth century, the family owned the Abercynrig estate near Brecon (Coflein, 2021), so they also had a Welsh connection.

Mary's father died on 27 June 1752 and was buried at Finglas (Vicars, 1908, p.196). Mary was only four years old, so she probably had very little memory of him. His titles and estate passed to his only son, William, who was born on 25 June 1744; he had had his eighth birthday just days before his father's death (Debrett, 1823, p.139). As the only heir, his inheritance would have been closely protected by his guardians until he became an adult — and likely until he had a son, ensuring the continuity of the family line.

In the event, William married on 9 March 1766, to Elizabeth Ridge. They had a son in 1767 when William was twenty-three; Mary Flower was then nineteen (ibid.).

With this, the male line was secured, and it is likely that little would have been provided for the sisters. For the middle and upper classes in the eighteenth century, a woman's wealth was the main factor for potential suitors, and the amount she brought to the union would be listed in the magazines and news sheets (Picard, 2000, pp.186–188) – which might explain why Elizabeth Flower, the middle child, never married, dying a spinster in 1813. At the time of Elizabeth's death, she was living on Charles Street, near Berkeley Square, in London (Cave, 1813, pp.388–9). Elizabeth would have been the "Hon. Miss Flower, &c." listed amongst the subscribers to *Poems, Lyrical and Pastoral*.

Her family seem to have had a relationship with the royal family; her nephew, the fourth Viscount Ashbrook, would later be appointed one of the Lords of the Bedchamber to King William IV (Mitford, 1847, p.83). It is not clear how close that relationship was in Mary's generation, but it may have been sufficient for her to win the Prince of Wales's patronage for Iolo – although we will meet another, perhaps more likely, candidate later on. Thus, when the Hon. Mary Nicholl and Iolo Morganwg fell out bitterly at the end of 1791 because of his republicanism, we can understand why. She had spent a year expending her social capital to introduce him to her network of aristocratic friends; in the list of subscribers to *Poems, Lyrical and Pastoral*, 59 sets were sold to titled patrons, and we can probably attribute most of these to Mary's efforts.

It seems that when she began her campaign to help Iolo, she had not been aware of his views towards the monarchy and the aristocracy. To her horror, she learned that he had been a supporter of the American Revolution and knew a number of leading American revolutionaries. Worse, he supported the French Revolution and the republican Jacobins (who, in late 1791, had not yet degenerated into their later violence): the enemy of everything her family stood for. While Mary Nicholl worked to win Iolo aristocratic patronage, he was publicly praising the republicans who were stripping power and status from the monarchy and aristocracy of France. This was enough to enrage her, and to lead to an exchange of angry letters between the two through the winter of 1791–2 (although some of Iolo's, at least, were written but never sent). But worse was to come. While Iolo struggled to get his poetry printed, the French Republic was established.

By the time he succeeded in publishing his work, Louis XVI, Marie Antoinette, the cream of the French aristocracy, the original Jacobin leadership, and tens of thousands of others had been executed. No wonder Mary was furious: while she had laboured on Iolo's behalf, he had been campaigning against the social structures which made her who she was. It has been assumed in the past that this was the end of the help she gave him, but, as we will see, this may not actually be the case.

Charnell-White (2009, p.377) refers to one of Iolo's unsent letters from January 1792, (NLW 21828IE Letter no. 224b), titled *Iolo Morganwg to an Aristocratic Woman* and adds the question, "Mrs Nicholl?". It seems very likely that it *was* Mrs Nicholl: Mary Nicholl was an aristocrat, born to a family of high rank. However, given that her family were relatively new in the aristocracy (hers was only the third generation, after all), and were Irish peers rather than English, she may well have been more insecure in her position, and more sensitive to Iolo's republicanism, than a member of a longer-established family would have been. Furthermore, as a younger daughter with no great inheritance, for most of her life, her name and her family's rank would have been her most valuable asset – hence the intensity of her anger.

Why, though, would an Irish aristocrat have invested so much effort in helping a lowly artisan-poet from Wales in the first place? To answer this question satisfactorily, we need to understand Iolo Morganwg's place amongst the gentry of Glamorgan, beginning with his mother and her parents.

3. Edward Mathew

Iolo's mother, Ann Matthews, was born in 1713 and died in 1770. Her father was Edward Mathew of Ty'n Caeau, Coychurch, just east of Bridgend – an area which was almost completely Welsh-speaking at that time (Jenkins, 1983, p.14). No record remains of her mother's name. Edward Mathew famously lost his family fortune and had to sell the family property, leaving Ann with no inheritance. Iolo, in his preface to *Poems, Lyrical and Pastoral*, describes him as "a gentleman who had wasted a pretty fortune".

Edward Mathew was a member of a family with a long history in Glamorgan. Nicholas (1874, p.120) describes them as "very ancient and long-continuing", extending back to Gwilym ap Gwaethfoed, Lord of Cardigan. Other, more recent, local historians (anon., 1991, p.20) say that the family descended from Aidan ap Gwaethfoed, who was Lord of Skenfrith, in Gwent. Both sources trace the Mathews' presence in Llandaff and Radyr back to one Ifan ap Gruffydd Gethin (ibid.; Nicholas, 1874, p.120), who settled in Llandaff: a village that, due to its cathedral, had city status. His son was Mathew Ifan Gruffydd, whose own son, David Mathew, became the first to use the English-style surname. In 1553, Miles Mathew bought the manor of Llandaff from the bishop, who was enriching himself by selling off so much of the diocesan property that it remained one of the poorest in Britain for centuries afterwards, with the cathedral ruinous for lack of funds to maintain it. Indeed, the diocese was so impoverished that no Bishop of Llandaff subsequently lived there until 1849, and they usually had to hold another post in England to survive. Meanwhile, they were unique amongst British bishops in that they no longer had the authority to appoint a single ecclesiastical living (Davies, 1962, p.69), those rights having been sold off. Miles Mathew's purchase included the official episcopal residence, the manor house of Bryn-y-gynnen, as well as substantial lands (Hilling, 1978, pp.33–35). The family intermarried widely with other prominent Glamorgan families and produced cadet branches in Radyr (just outside Cardiff), Castell-y-Mynach (near Llantrisant), and elsewhere, which became important in their own right (ibid., pp.120-121). Until the Reformation, all of the branches of the family were strong supporters of the Catholic pilgrim trail from Llandaff to "Our Lady of Penrhys" in the Rhondda valley (anon., 1991, p.21; Ahmed, 2022).

The Llandaff branch of the family had a long association with the military. Sir David Mathew was standard-bearer to Edward of Westminster at the Battle of Towton in 1461, in which the House of York crushed the House of Lancaster in a vast and bloody battle. The victory established Edward as the new King of England: Edward IV, replacing the defeated Henry VI. Sir David's death was less glorious: he was killed in a riot at Neath (Evans, 1943, p.283) by the Turbervilles three years later (anon., 1991, p.20). He had married the heiress of Gloucestershire's le Vele family (Hilling, 1975, p.64). A generation later, Sir William Mathew was knighted by Henry VII of the now-victorious Lancastrians on the field of Bosworth (Evans, 1943, p.283). He was a much-appreciated patron of the bards of Glamorgan (anon., 1991, p.22). His eldest son, George, was the Sheriff of Glamorgan in 1554, and briefly the county's Member of Parliament in 1554; he was knighted in 1554 (Williams, 1895, p.95). The family produced a Governor-in-Chief of the British possessions in the Caribbean, William Mathew, who was appointed to the post in 1703 and became an admiral in 1704 (Hilling, 1975, p.74).

A second admiral, and one of the leaders of the Whig faction in the county, was Thomas Mathew (Evans, 1943, p.73; Thomas, n.d.), whose father Edward was a brigadier general (Williams, 1895, p.100). Born in 1670, he was described as hot-tempered and quarrelsome and was known as a very strict disciplinarian. Entering the navy in 1703 – the year when, as we shall see, the downfall of his relative Edward, Iolo Morganwg's grandfather, was set in motion – he went on to have a career filled with glorious successes (Williams, 1852, pp.316–7). In 1744, at 74 years of age, he had Bryn-y-gynnen rebuilt and renamed Llandaff Court (Hilling, 1975, p.41). In December of the same year, he also commanded a British fleet in battle against the combined forces of France and Spain. His second-in-command failed to join in the attack, leading to its failure, and the acrimonious aftermath led to Mathews being court-martialled and dismissed from the navy in 1747 – something that led to public protests (Williams, 1852, pp.316–7). The controversy seems not to have slowed him down; he was elected the MP for Glamorgan shortly after the battle, on 2 January 1745, and held the seat until 1747, when he became instead the Member for Carmarthenshire (Williams, 1895, p.100). He died in 1751, at Pencoed, in the parish of Coychurch, where his relative Edward Mathew had once lived. He was apparently not a popular man in Cardiff; Evans (1943, p.156) quotes a contemporary rhyme in Welsh satirising his seemingly insatiable avarice. His son, Thomas William Mathews, had been an army major but resigned when his father was expelled from the navy. He followed his father as the Member of Parliament for Glamorgan between 1756 and 1761 (Williams, 1895, p.101; Thomas, n.d.).

The Radyr branch, meanwhile, were more business-minded, though not more peaceful. Sir William Mathew was knighted in 1515 and died in either 1528 or 1529; his son, George, was knighted in 1553 and died in 1558 (Robinson, 1987, pp.292–293). By the end of the sixteenth century, the family had built an iron-smelting works at Pentyrch where they produced firearms and iron for the export market (Hilling, 1975, pp.67–68). Such exports were illegal, but when agents of the king, James I, attempted to confiscate some of his lands, Edmund Mathew, his family, and a heavily armed band of over one hundred followers put up such a violent resistance that the king's men concluded that they could not win without cannon – which they did not have. Deciding that discretion was the better part of valour, they withdrew and never returned (Evans, 1943, pp.93-94). This was no late blemish on Edmund's name; earlier in his career, during the reign of Elizabeth, he had been the Sheriff of Glamorgan and had been the subject of legal action by the Crown for abusing the position to enrich himself, and for starting riots (ibid., p.394). Although Edmund seems to have escaped unpunished for his defiance of royal authority, the Mathews of Radyr were soon gone: Edmund's son, George, sold the estate in 1625 and moved to Ireland (anon., 1991, pp.32–33). During Iolo's lifetime, the descendants of the Radyr Mathews became members of the Irish peerage, choosing the title of Baron (later Earl) of Llandaff, on the basis that they still owned some property there (Williams, 1996, p.66).

This temperament continued into later generations: an Anthony Mathew of Leckwith is recorded as being part of an attempt to break a man out of prison during the mid-eighteenth century (Moore, 1975, p.128). The family had therefore been both important and notorious in Glamorgan for many generations by Edward Mathew's time and continued to be so during the life of his grandson, Iolo Morganwg.

As for Edward Mathew himself, little is known about him or his branch of the family. Rice Merrick, writing in between 1578 and 1584, recorded that one Thomas Mathew had lived in Bryncwtyn, two miles from Ty'n Caeau, at least four generations earlier, and had sold that property to Thomas ap Rosser Fychan (James, 1983, p.105); whether this was the same branch of the family is unclear. Edwards (2009, p.109) suggests that Edward Mathew may have been a good poet. Like his relatives, he is known to have had a hot temper, and Williams (1956, p.87) records that he was excommunicated for fighting in a churchyard but successfully appealed against the penalty. So how did he come to lose everything?

Jenkins (2012, p.11) ascribes it to "profligacy or misfortune", which fits Iolo's description from *Poems*, but there is another intriguing possibility. Elsewhere, Iolo says of his grandfather that he was competent but had been forced to sell his property due partly to bad luck, but in greater part because of the malice of others (Williams, 1956, p.88). This is a different narrative, implying that Edward Mathew was not the author of his own downfall.

There is some surviving evidence that suggests who Iolo may have had in mind. Two documents held by the National Library of Wales (Penrice and Margam Estate Records, documents 2670 and 3887) refer to a legal case brought in 1703 against "Edward Mathew, assessor and collector of the land tax for the lower hamlet of Coychurch, co. Glam". This is very probably Iolo's grandfather. He was charged with failing to collect "a land tax for carrying on the war", found guilty, and ordered to pay a fine of £20. The case was brought by "Sir Edward Mansell and others". Unfortunately, the document detailing the case (Penrice and Margam 3887) has gone missing from the library's archives (Davies, 2021), but the catalogue entries contain the relevant information for both documents.

Jenkins (1983, pp.45–47) highlights the difficulties of obtaining accurate details of the incomes of the gentry but, using data collected by the same Edward Mansell in 1677, he shows that in that year, the estate of the Matthews family of Llandaff generated an income of £400. The Matthews family of Aberaman (near Aberdare in the Rhondda) had an income of £500, and the Matthews of Castell-y-Mynach (Llantrisant) an income of £700. He concludes (pp.48–49) that a typical gentleman from a "secondary" family would have an annual income of between £150 and £350. The lowest group of gentry families had an income of £50–£200, and Edward Mathew probably fell into this group, since Morgan (2011, p.127) describes him simply as "a farmer". This is supported by the 1670 Hearth Tax returns for Glamorgan, which listed by name everyone who was wealthy enough to have a chimney (the common folk, who lived in thatched cottages, did not). In that year, only one Mathew is listed in the parish of Coychurch: George Mathew of Pencoed, whose home had two hearths (Parkinson, 1994, p.42). This is a far cry from "David Mathews Esq." of Bryn-y-Gynnen, Llandaff, who had 13 hearths, or "Thomas Mathew Esq." of Castell-yn-Mynach, who had ten, in the same year (ibid., p.xxxii). The Coychurch Mathews were clearly not overly prosperous.

The gentry of Glamorgan tended to spend money freely and accumulate large debts; Jenkins goes on to describe (1983, p.67) a family which, in 1739, had an annual income of £2,000 but which could barely afford to buy necessities. During the seventeenth century, one member of the Castell-y-Mynach branch of the Mathews family, Humphrey Mathews, had been prepared to pay the huge sum of £500 for a collection of manuscripts for his library (Heal & Holmes, 1994, p.280). It is unlikely that this money came from savings, but rather was borrowed. Such spending was, though, regarded as necessary to "keep up appearances" and demonstrate one's status (ibid.). In this period, borrowing usually worked on the basis of rolling short-term loans; long-term loans were rare. This being the case, should lenders become concerned about a debtor's financial prospects – which might very well have been the case once it became known that Edward Mathews was a target of the Mansells – the supply of fresh loans might dry up, with full repayment demanded (ibid., p.161).

Furthermore, the finances of families such as the Castell-y-Mynach Mathews had been significantly undermined after 1696. In that year, the Mint declared all "clipped" coinage to be invalid and began reissuing new coins. Much of the stored wealth of this rural branch of the Mathews family consisted of such old, clipped coins, and the value of this was now significantly in doubt (Thomas, 2005, pp.71–72). This estate was close to the Coychurch estate of Edward Mathew, and he had been similarly affected by this law. The penalty of £20 imposed on Edward Mathew would therefore have been a very significant financial blow; it may be that others followed, for which the records have been lost. His later crisis had been set in motion ten years before his daughter's birth.

Why would Mansell have brought this case against Edward Mathew? It is important to understand the context.

In 1703, the British government's main form of direct taxation was a tax on the value of land, instituted in 1698 (Beckett, 1985, p.285), and a Window Tax (1696), which replaced the previous Hearth Tax (ibid., p.298). This was mostly paid by the aristocracy, and by the gentry – who found it extremely burdensome. The land tax was often one shilling on the pound, but when the country was at war (as it was in 1703), it could rise to four shillings on the pound (Hill, 1977, p.147). With 20 shillings to the pound, this was a 20% tax.

The case brought against Iolo's grandfather specifically mentions a "tax to pay for the war" – the war in question being the War of the Spanish Succession, which had begun in 1701 and was to last until 1714, the year after Ann Mathew's birth. This saw military spending absorb two-thirds of all government expenditure (Beckett & Turner, 1990, p.397), which mostly came from taxation of the gentry. In this period, the land tax was the highest it had been for half a century (ibid., p.386).

Edward Mathew would thus have been charged with levying large sums of money to pay for an unpopular war from landowners who were already in very considerable financial straits, and who were very vocally complaining that the taxes were ruining them (Jenkins, 1983, p.141). Landowners – the gentry – might have tried to fund their tax payments by increasing their tenants' rent but they often were unable to do so, meaning that they had to pay the tax from their own resources (ibid., p.385) – Edward Mathew included.

These issues were common throughout England and Wales, but as a tax collector in Glamorgan, Edward Mathew was also operating in the midst of high-stakes local politics.

In the eighteenth century, the structure of government was largely what it had been in Tudor times; the civil service as we think of it today did not exist until the middle of the nineteenth century (Civil Service Commission, n.d.). Assessment of the amounts to be paid was performed by assessors who answered ultimately to the king, rather than to Parliament (Beckett, 1985, p.292). However, appointment to the position was the gift of the local Justices of the Peace. This position had been established in Wales by Henry VIII and had far more power than it does today (Williams, 1919, pp.80–81). Indeed, the local Justices were effectively a law unto themselves, with almost no oversight of their activities (Twiston Davies & Edwards, 1939, p.23; Thomas, 1976, p.20). Until 1693, there was a maximum of eight Justices for each county (Williams, 1919, p.79), and between them they performed the functions that today would be the responsibility of local councils – including the appointment of a host of local officials (ibid., p.81), including tax assessors, customs inspectors, and the livings of local parishes (Thomas, 1976, p.20). These posts were frequently given to family members or political supporters who would use their powers to increase their personal wealth, improve their social status, and influence the chances of their success in legal cases (Jenkins, 1983, p.69).

Quotas for the taxes to be raised were set for each county by the government, but it was up to the local assessors to decide how this sum should be raised. They could do it as they saw fit, and that made it lucrative since, although they were not paid for the role, they could claim a portion of the taxes raised (Thomas, 1976, p.22). There was great opportunity for the enhancement of personal wealth (Jenkins, 1982, p.158), which may not have been unrelated to the fact that the taxation values of estates were often set suspiciously low; the assessors' oaths as to the accuracy of their figures were not held in high regard by the government but were nevertheless accepted in order to ensure regular collection (Beckett, 1985, p.301). No doubt "incentives" might be provided for a lower assessment. Over a century passed after the land tax had been introduced before Parliament tried to find out what methods were being used to raise it in different parts of the kingdom (ibid., p.295).

All of this, however, would make a tax assessor a target. Should an opposing faction or family rise to power in a county, they would want to appoint their own man. Furthermore, Edward Mathew may have been appointed before the war began in 1701, which had been at a time of relatively low taxation. By 1703, the increase of taxation to 20% had opened up far greater opportunities for enrichment; greedy eyes would have been eyeing the opportunity.

In that year, Glamorgan was embroiled in intense, and frequently violent, power struggles waged between a bewildering array of factions. These are too complex to go into here but are discussed in detail by Jenkins (1983, pp.134–141). At the centre of it all was the rise to dominance of the Mansell family of Margam, led by Sir Edward Mansell (1634 –1706). He had been a prominent supporter of King William III, the Dutch-born William of Orange (Jenkins, 1983, p.142), at a time when many, even those who were not necessarily Jacobite supporters of the deposed Stuart dynasty, were opposed to having a foreign-born king. This reluctance to support William's successors, the German-born Hanoverians, lasted until the middle of the eighteenth century, when George III, the first of the dynasty actually to have been born in Britain, took the throne (Thomas, 1960, p.100).

In his campaign to dominate Glamorgan politics, Mansell could be ruthless. For example, in 1705 he was accused of attempting to cripple the business of his coal-mining competitor – Sir Humphrey Mackworth's Mine Adventurers' Company – by abusing his position as a Justice of the Peace to forcibly conscript a number of Mackworth's employees into the army. Mansell's servants were also accused of assaulting a government official, the Portreeve of Neath (Twiston Davies & Edwards, 1939, p.92) – essentially, the mayor of the borough (Jones, 1984, p.75). Frivolous lawsuits were brought against public officials on the grounds that they spoke no English, only Welsh; in other cases, simply because they preferred Welsh to English despite speaking both languages (Mackworth, 1707, p.5). This was widespread behaviour at the time, and it was common for the gentry to ignore or abuse the law (Jenkins, 1983, p.91). It was this Edward Mansell who brought a lawsuit against Edward Mathew.

Edward Mansell died in 1706, but this would not have improved the situation for Edward Mathew: Mansell's son Thomas was just as likely to use any and all means to break opponents, regardless of the law (Mackworth, 1707). Thomas Mansell was made a baron in 1711, having previously been Queen Anne's Comptroller of the Household, a privy councillor, and a Treasury commissioner (Burke, 1838, p.339). He became so powerful that his enemies amongst the landed gentry increasingly gave up the struggle (Jenkins, 1983, p.149), and he used this power to give office to his supporters (ibid., p.149). Meanwhile, Humphrey Mackworth, the bitter enemy of the Mansells, was himself acquiring immense political and economic power. The battle between the two was ferocious and was fought on multiple fronts as the two factions sought to appoint their own candidates to key legal and government posts and to get rid of the other side's appointees (ibid., p.59). If Edward Mansell had targeted Edward Mathew, his son is likely to have continued the campaign.

This suggests that Edward Mathew, rather than being profligate or merely unfortunate, was in fact one of the casualties in a vicious conflict between different factions of the gentry, and that the loss of his property was due to the abuse of power by nobles close to the monarchy. If so, it is likely that Iolo Morganwg's lifelong hatred of powerful grandees, of the abuse of power, and of the monarchy, had its roots in his grandfather's downfall.

4. The Edwins

It is surprising that past biographies of Iolo Morganwg have rarely discussed what happened to Edward Mathew after he sold his estate. His wife died in the same year, and he was unable to support his daughter, so he sent her to his sister-in-law – but he was still alive. What became of him?

The only biographer to answer this question is Williams (1956, p.88), who indicates that Edward Mathew became a tenant farmer renting land from the Edwin family of Llanmihangel.

If this is the case, then it shines further light on patterns that were formed during Edward Mathews' life which then re-emerged in the life of his grandson, Iolo Morganwg. To make this clear, an overview of the Edwin family will help.

Llanmihangel Place is an outstanding example of Elizabethan architecture. It sits on the upper slopes of a hill near the hamlet of Siginstone, which is just off the main road between Cowbridge and Llantwit Major. At the bottom of the hill, overlooked from the main windows at the front of the manor house, is a small church.

The estate had been the property of the Thomas family, who had once been one of the wealthiest families in Glamorgan. However, the last of them to own Llanmihangel, Sir Robert Thomas, had been a man of extraordinarily bad judgement and no great character who had become deeply mired in debt. He was forced to sell his manor and lands to one of his creditors, Humphrey Edwin (Thomas, 1997, pp.15–18).

Edwin was a London merchant with Welsh family roots (Jenkins, 1959a). He bought Llanmihangel in 1685, paying the sum of £12,812 – the money coming from the sale of his shares in the East India Company (Thomas, 1997, p.20). Shortly afterwards, in 1687, he was knighted and appointed Sheriff of Glamorgan (Jenkins, 1959a). However, his entry in the *Dictionary of Welsh Biography* seems inaccurate: although he was appointed, he did not serve. The actual sheriff that year was, in a curious twist, Edward Mansel of Margam (Nicholas, 1874, p.142). Edwin was excused the obligation (Moore, 1995, p.90) – something repeated when he was appointed but excused in 1704, with Robert Jones of Fonmon Castle, who was his son-in-law (ibid., p.91; Williams, 1966, p.49), taking on the role instead. This was common in the seventeenth and eighteenth centuries, as will be discussed later, but in 1687 it is likely that power politics were at play, given that Mansel and Edwin were so opposed religiously and politically. Edwin maintained his business activities in the capital and, in 1697, became the Lord Mayor of London (Jenkins, 1959a); as mayor, he was one of the people who greeted William of Orange when he arrived in England to become king (Williams, 1966, pp.47-49). Sir Humphrey was a prominent non-conformist (Jenkins, 1983, p.180), and caused something of a scandal by attending Dissenting meetings in his mayoral regalia. This had provoked the Tories in Parliament into strengthening laws discriminating against religious non-conformists (anon., 2004). It is likely that, having become involved in the affairs of Glamorgan, he, as a Whig and Dissenter, would have been strongly opposed to the Tory and High Church Thomas Mansell. He died at Llanmihangel on 14 December 1707, a few years after Edward Mathew's troubles began, and was buried in the ancient church next door to the manor house.

Sir Humphrey's son and heir, Samuel (born in December 1671), moved away from his father's radical religious beliefs, and back towards the Established Church (Thomas, 1997, p.24). The family's rise in social status, and their return to religious respectability, led to Samuel marrying the daughter of the Earl of Manchester, Lady Catherine Montagu. Samuel Edwin died in 1722, the year in which Edward Mathew lost his estate, and was buried in Llanmihangel Church with his parents. Lady Catherine died in 1731 and was likewise buried in Llanmihangel.

After Samuel's death, Llanmihangel passed to his son Charles, who had been born in or around 1699 (Jenkins, 1959a). He had recently achieved his majority, so it was probably Charles who leased land to Edward Mathew. Charles was appointed Sheriff of Glamorgan in 1725 but, like his father, was excused, with one Abraham Barbour appointed instead (Moore, 1995, p.91). Charles went on to become the MP for Westminster in 1742, serving for one term of Parliament. He later became the MP for Glamorgan from 1747 until 1756, the year of his death. He also married well: his wife was Lady Charlotte Hamilton, daughter of the 4th Duke of Hamilton. The couple did not have any children so, upon Charles Edwin's death, the estate passed to his sister's eldest son, Charles Wyndham. However, the will specified that he could only come into the inheritance after the death of Lady Charlotte; he had to wait a long time, as she lived until 1777 (Thomas, 1997, pp.24–25). In that year, Iolo Morganwg was thirty years old. Lady Charlotte's time in Llanmihangel is worth noting since, while she was firmly attached to the Church of England, she was an early and leading advocate of Methodism (Jenkins, 1959), as her mother-in-law Lady Catherine had also been (Williams, 1966, p.49), and she used her power of patronage to appoint a number of Methodist ministers to the livings of parishes on the Edwin estates (Jenkins, 1954, p.188; Sanders, n.d.)

Reviewing the Edwin family tree is useful for several reasons.

Firstly, it establishes that Edward Mathew, ruined by the Mansells, may well have been sheltered by a family which had political and religious reasons for opposing the Mansell faction. It means that Edward Mathew would have been able to be an ongoing presence in his daughter's life even after she had been taken in at Boverton.

Secondly, we know that Iolo Morganwg's early career as a poet grew out of his friendship with a group of bards in the northern uplands of Glamorgan (Lewis, 2009, pp.72–73). Two of them, Dafydd Nicolas and John Bradford, were older; how Iolo came to know them will be discussed later. Others were closer to his own age – but how did Iolo, from the Vale lowlands, meet them? As it happens, the Llanmihangel estate was a very large one: it had contained land in Flemingston since the mid-sixteenth century (Thomas, 1997, p.10) and a great deal of land in *Tir*

Iarll and the Welsh-speaking Glamorgan uplands since the early seventeenth century – in fact, it amounted to over 18,000 acres (ibid., p.11). Given the Edwins' piety and religious activism, they would have wanted stonemasons to work on their domestic and religious properties. It is reasonable to speculate that they commissioned works from Edward Williams, a stonemason and builder living near their Flemingston properties and, later, from Edward's sons, who were all stonemasons in the family enterprise. Since religious monuments are something very personal, requiring some discussion of inscription and design, it must be considered likely that Charles and, particularly, Lady Charlotte Edwin knew both Iolo's grandfather and father, as well as Iolo himself, and that Iolo's journeys to *Tir Iarll* were at least partly to execute commissions for the Edwin family.

Thirdly, Samuel Edwin's wife, Lady Catherine Montagu, had, before her marriage, been a lady-in-waiting to Queen Caroline – the consort of King George II (who had made Mary Nicholl's father a viscount), and grandmother of King George III (Thomas, 1997, p.22). In the next generation, Charles Edwin's wife, Lady Charlotte Hamilton, had been a Lady of the Bedchamber to Princess Augusta, the Dowager Princess of Wales (ibid., p.25). Princess Augusta of Saxe-Coburg had married Frederick, Prince of Wales and son of George II and Queen Caroline, in 1736. Their son, the future King George III, was born in 1737. However, Frederick died suddenly in 1751, while his son was still a minor. If George II had died before his grandson became an adult, Augusta would have become regent and played a role in the government of the kingdom, with Lady Charlotte as one of her closest confidantes. In the event, this did not happen, and George was already an adult when he became king in 1760 (Bullion, 2004). However, this means that the Edwins of Llanmihangel had a close personal relationship with two generations of the monarchy.

Fourth, as noted, after Samuel Edwin's death, the property passed to his nephew: Charles Wyndham. On receiving his inheritance, Charles changed his surname to Edwin and went on to become the MP for Glamorgan from 1780 to 1789. When he stood down, his son stood for election in his place (Jenkins, 1959a). The son, Thomas, used his father's original surname – and in the passionate election campaign of 1789, Thomas Wyndham received the celebrated support of Iolo Morganwg, the Mathew family, and others who are significant in Iolo's story, as we shall see later.

Finally, Llanmihangel Place is only two and a half miles from Boverton Place. Edward's daughter, Ann Matthews, Iolo's mother, was nine years old when her father finally lost everything in 1722. She was taken in, Iolo said, by the family of Richard Seys of Boverton, who had married her maternal aunt (Williams, 1975, p.91). The Seys family were very important amongst the Glamorgan gentry, and they would have known their near neighbours, Charles and Lady Charlotte Edwin, well. The Edwins knew Edward Mathew, who was one of their tenant farmers. Charles lived to see Ann Matthews married, settled, and have children; Lady Charlotte lived to see those children grow to maturity. Ann Matthews and her aunt were thus well-acquainted with a family which had strong royal connections. Who were Ann's mother and aunt, though? What was their background?

5. Ann Matthew's Mother and Aunt

Ann's mother appears to have disappeared completely from history; none of Iolo's biographers have been able to name her. Her aunt has been misidentified, as we shall see. However, there are some pointers to their identity and background.

Williams (1975, p.92) repeats Iolo's own account of his mother's early years. She had been educated, Iolo says, and this had been paid for by her "Cousin German", who was a daughter of Richard Seys. This cousin was the sister of Lady King (Peter, Baron King, being the Lord High Chancellor of England), and this same cousin had married her own "cousin German" who was heir to Boverton via entail. He gives this cousin's surname as being initially "Seys" through this marriage, and "Price" through remarriage.

"Cousin German", in contemporary English "cousin-german", specifically means a first cousin (www.collinsdictionary.com, n.d.), rather than "cousin" in a more general sense, which is used to mean a relative within the extended family (dictionary.cambridge.

org, n.d.). Therefore, Iolo is being very precise here: his mother's education was funded by a female first cousin whose husband was also her own first cousin. We will be able to identify exactly who this was below. However, the cousin concerned was not the sister of Lady King – or at least, not in the sense that we would understand it today. This is made clear via a "Pedigree of the Seys Family" published in two parts in the *Cardiff and Merthyr Guardian* in July 1863 (anon., 1863a, 1863b).

The Seys family had been in Boverton since the sixteenth century when Roger Seys married Elizabeth Voss, who had been a maid of honour to Queen Elizabeth. Since their family tree will be important in more than one part of our story, it is worth reviewing it in some detail.

Boverton Place was believed to have been given to Elizabeth's ancestor, Griffith Voss, as a reward for assistance he had provided to Jasper Tudor, the uncle of the first Tudor king, Henry VII (James, 1975, p.212). Jasper was Lord of Glamorgan from 1486 to 1495, and Griffith supposedly provided a place of refuge to him at a time of great danger. It was popularly said that the manor had previously been a place of hiding for King John as he tried to avoid signing the Magna Carta (Evans, 1943, p.204); it was the property of his first wife, Hawise (also known as Isabel), daughter of the Earl of Gloucester, whom he had arbitrarily divorced. Nevertheless, she gave him shelter under the pseudonym of Gerald Fitzgerald (Morris, 1907, p.161) or Gilbert Fitzallan (Robertson Spencer, 1913, p.127).

Elizabeth Voss had inherited Boverton Place as there were no male children in her generation. Roger Seys and Elizabeth had two sons. The eldest, and their heir, was Richard, who married Mary Evans.

Richard and Mary, who had eleven children, will be our reference point. The first child was a son, Roger, who, for some reason, which he must have long regretted afterwards, struck his mother – for which he was disinherited (Gibbs, 1971, p.25). The second son, now the heir, was Evan. The third son was another Richard, whom I will refer to as Richard (II). The remaining children are not relevant to our understanding of Iolo's story. Roger, however, will be further discussed later in the narrative.

Evan inherited Boverton Place and had three children: a son, Richard, and two daughters: Elizabeth and Margaret. I will refer to this Richard as Richard (III). On his father's death, he became the owner of the estate, but his inheritance was conditional. An entail in Evan's will stipulated that Boverton must always pass to a male relative; should the male line fail in the branch of the family which owned Boverton, the ownership would move to another branch (anon., 1863b). This was intended to rule out the possibility of the property being inherited by a woman and leaving the family through marriage, as had happened with the Voss family, and was a very common practice among the Glamorgan gentry (Jones, 1976, p.38).

Richard (III) had four children – Evan, William, Ann, and Margaret – and died in 1714. William, who lived in Llanrhidian, predeceased his father, dying in 1710 with no heirs (Nicholas, 1874, p.124).

Ann married in 1704, to Peter King who would become 1st Baron King and Lord Chancellor of England. She was born in 1688 or 1689 and died in 1767 (Lemmings, 2004). Ann, Lady King, was thus the daughter of Richard (III). Margaret never married.

Richard (III)'s son Evan now inherited Boverton Place. Two documents held by the Glamorgan

Archives (DF/D/719 and DTRE/382, 383), identifying him as the son and heir of Richard Seys of Boverton, report him as engaging in business in Cowbridge in September 1719. However, the 1863 genealogy says that he died no later than 1720, so his death must have come very shortly after this. He also had no children and was therefore the last male of his direct line to live at Boverton (anon., 1863b).

The entail in Evan's will now came into effect, and the estate was transferred to the line of Richard (II), the third son of Richard and Mary. He had five children: the ones of interest here are William, and his younger brother, another Richard – Richard (IV) (ibid.).

William had two sons: Charles, the elder, and Evan. William did not live much longer than Richard (III) since he died in 1715, although his will was not proven until 1724. It was probably contested, because the entire estate was left to Evan, the younger son. Charles was bequeathed a mere £5 (ibid.).

Meanwhile, Richard (IV) had married a widow, Wenllian, who had previously been married to a Thomas Price. They had one child: a daughter, Elizabeth (ibid.).

Boverton Place now became the property of Evan, the son of William. The anonymous author of the 1863 pedigree is unsure exactly how this happened: either Richard Seys (III) left the property to William, and Evan inherited upon William's death according to William's will; or Richard Seys (III) left the property to Richard Seys (IV), and it passed to Evan when Richard Seys (IV) died without a male heir. The author considers the second more likely but is not sure whether Richard Seys (IV) and his wife Wenllian ever actually lived at Boverton (ibid.).

In fact, they did. The National Library of Wales has a legal document (NLW 3816-3817) identifying both Wenllian as the widow of Richard Seys of Boverton and Elizabeth as Richard's daughter. This shows that Richard (IV) did indeed take up residence at Boverton.

Elizabeth Seys, daughter of Richard Seys (IV) and Wenllian, married her first cousin Evan – the son of William – and so, when Richard (IV) died (the date is unclear), Evan and Elizabeth took ownership of Boverton Place. There was a large age gap between them; Evan was much older than his wife, who was born in 1707 (Morgan, 2011, p.127). When he died in 1733 with no children, his will allowed Elizabeth to occupy the property for the rest of her life.

However, the actual ownership of the property was inherited by a male relative from a different branch of the Seys family, also called Evan, whose own son died at the age of seventeen. There seem to have been no remaining male heirs anywhere in the Seys family at this point, and so the ownership of Boverton Place passed to Evan's daughter Jane, who married Robert Jones of Fonmon Castle, a short distance away. She died without children. There was then a legal battle over the ownership (James, 1975, p.218), but in 1774, Jones became Boverton's owner (anon., 1863b) and the property finally left the Seys family.

Elizabeth Seys lived a long life, until 1785 (Morgan, 2011, p.127), and married twice more whilst living at Boverton: to Lewis Price, and then to a man named Blades. Neither Elizabeth nor Robert Jones seem to have had any motive at this point to spend money on maintaining Boverton Place; the ancient house fell into disrepair and was completely in ruins well before Iolo Morganwg died in 1826 (James, 1975, p.218). The ruins were dismantled to build a farmhouse nearby; during this work, a riding boot full of guineas was found concealed in one of the walls (Robertson Spencer, 1913, p.128).

This sets the context for us to understand the household into which Ann Matthews came to live. The Richard Seys who was the head of the household at that time was Richard Seys (IV). His wife, therefore Ann's aunt, was called Wenllian. Unfortunately, the 1863 pedigree only gives her previous married name, Price, not her maiden name.

Williams (1975, p.92) quotes a letter sent to Iolo in 1784. It was written by "Elisa Blades late price of Boverton", who greets Iolo with "Dr Cousin" and signs the letter "Your loveing [sic] Aunt". This seems to be the basis for Jenkins' assertion that Ann's aunt was "Elizabeth Blades" (2018, p.37), "née Seys" (2012, p.11). However, the 1863 pedigree matches Iolo's description precisely, making it clear that this Elizabeth was in fact Ann Mathew's cousin, and was only one generation older than Iolo. "Aunt" conveys the age difference, while "cousin" is used in the more general sense of "relative". Elizabeth died in 1785, a year after sending that letter.

Wenllian did not take the main responsibility for her young niece. Iolo's description makes it clear that Ann's education was paid for by Elizabeth, not by Richard and Wenllian, while the 1784 letter – written the year before Elizabeth's death – indicates that Elizabeth had maintained a lifelong relationship with Ann's son: Iolo.

This makes sense. Richard may still have been alive when Ann arrived in Boverton, but he did not have much longer to live. The document referred to above, which proves that Richard and Wenllian did live in Boverton Place, actually refers to a case brought by a gentleman (that is, a member of the gentry) living in Cardiff, one Thomas Rice. Wenllian is referred to not only as the widow of Richard Seys of Boverton but also as the wife of this Thomas Rice; Elizabeth is also mentioned and is identified as the daughter of Richard and Wenllian. The document seems to have been written in the 1720s.

Thus, within a few years of Ann arriving in Boverton, Richard (IV) had died. His estate, according to the entail on the property, would have been inherited by a male of the next generation, not by his wife or daughter – which is to say, Richard's nephew Evan, who had married Richard's daughter, Elizabeth. Wenllian, Ann's maternal aunt, may have been left some bequest but it is unlikely to have been substantial, so within a short time, she had remarried. The 1863 pedigree says that she died in May 1750 at the age of 87 (anon., 1863b); she would therefore have been born in or around 1663 and lived to see Ann married. As we will see, it is probable that she returned to live in Boverton at some point after her remarriage.

There is one more indication of where the identity of Ann Matthew's mother and aunt might be found, which for some reason seems not to have been explored to date. Iolo's friend and biographer, Elijah Waring (1850, p.9), recounts an anecdote from Iolo's youth. Having been chastised by his father for reading when he should have been working, Iolo put his books in a bag and walked away. His father observed, "Now Neddy will go to his mother's people at Aberpergwm, and Pontneddfychan, and will pout for a week or two, and then we shall see him again."

"His mother's people" either refers to Ann Mathew's father's family, or her mother's. It is unlikely to have been the former since, as we have already seen, the Mathew family were concentrated towards the south and east of the county. Aberpergwm, near Neath in western Glamorgan, was the seat of the Williams family – one of the few families amongst the Glamorgan gentry who continued to speak Welsh, and who were patrons of Welsh-language culture (Jenkins, 1959b). We now know that Ann Mathew's aunt was Wenllian: a Welsh name, at a time when the Glamorgan gentry had increasingly switched to using English.

The Williams family had been at Aberpergwm for hundreds of years, going back to Jenkin ap William ap Jenkin ap Hopkin (Nicholas, 1874, p.189) and, ultimately, to Iestyn ap Gwrgant, the Welsh Lord of Glamorgan defeated by Fitzhamon (Williams, 1966, p.87). They claimed descent from Dafydd Gam, Owain Glyndwr's bitter enemy, who died on the field of Agincourt (ibid.). During the Civil War, they had been strong supporters of the king (Oak, 1974, p.72). However, they were believed to be connected with the family from whom Oliver Cromwell was descended: his ancestor Morgan Williams was from Glamorgan, though from Whitchurch (near Llandaff, where one branch of the Mathew family were located), and Cromwell himself sometimes used the name Williams, even during his time as Lord Protector of the Commonwealth (Nicholas, 1874, pp.131–2; Morrill, 2004). This relationship was supposed to be the reason why Cromwell's army had spared Aberpergwm when other Royalist estates had been destroyed or expropriated (Oak, 1974, p.72).

The Williamses were well-connected (Jenkins, 1983, pp.32–35), and they were neighbours of Humphrey

Mackworth, who began pioneering coal production on his Gnoll estate in 1690 (Twiston Davies & Edwards, 1939, p.91). As the dispute grew between Mackworth and Edward Mansell, at the time when Mansell brought his lawsuit against Iolo's grandfather, where would they have stood? Certainly, they had themselves been exploiting the coal reserves on their own property since at least 1670 (Jenkins, 1953, p.961; Thomas, 1974, p.181), so it is likely they were also opposed to Mansell.

In the Glamorgan election of 1789, the Williams family of Aberpergwm were on the same side as the Mathews family, supported strongly by Iolo, in securing the election of Thomas Wyndham, the candidate supported by the local county gentry, most of whom lived on their estates, over a candidate supported by titled, aristocratic landowners, who were generally absentee landlords. Wyndham's supporters included (emphasis added):

"**Matthews, of Llandaff**; Powell, of Llanharran; Price, of Dyffryn, and Jenkins, of Pantynawel. Thomas, of Pwllywrach; Popkin, of Talygarn**; Deere**, of Penlline; Aubrey of Llantryddid, Gwyn, of Llansanor; Picton of Lutton; Knight, of Tythegstone; Rees, of Court Colman; Miss Gwinnett, of Penlline; **Williams, of Aberpergwm**; Gough, Ynyscedwyn; Rous, Courtyralla; Bassett, of Bonvilston; etc., etc. These were the principal supporters of Wyndham, 'When he nobly for liberty stood.'" (Cadrawd, 1904, p.1)

The election came after the long-term MP for Glamorgan, Charles Edwin, stood down; the new MP, Thomas Wyndham, was his son (Jenkins, 1983, p.188). This, of course, was the Edwin family from whom Iolo's grandfather had rented land. It is also worth mentioning that Humphrey Mackworth's grandson,

Sir Herbert Mackworth, MP for Cardiff between 1766 and 1790, was one of the subscribers to Iolo's *Poems, Lyrical and Pastoral*: another hint of a continuing family connection.

There are numerous indications that Iolo and the Williams family of Aberpergwm were at the very least associated. They took an interest in the contemporary English cultural scene, and one of them, Rees, is recorded as corresponding in 1802 with Iolo Morganwg's friend, the poet Robert Southey (Jenkins, 1954, p.961), at a time when Southey was still a political radical. More significantly, it was also this family who had brought the poet Dafydd Nicolas into their household as a tutor; this happened around the middle of the eighteenth century (Williams, 1959b; Lewis, 2004b), so it would have been approximately the time of Iolo's birth. Nicolas was later an important influence on Iolo's development as a poet in Welsh. If Iolo regularly went to his mother's relatives in Aberpergwm for weeks at a stretch, as Waring implies, was it to spend time with Nicolas?

I have not been able to find a detailed family tree of the Williams family, but further research in the Williams family's papers at the National Library of Wales may be able to establish whether one of the daughters of the family was a (G)wenllian, born around 1663. If so, it may also be possible to finally identify and give a name to Ann Matthews' mother. The Seys and Mathew families were important; the women they married would have come from families of similar status, and the Williams family certainly fit the profile.

Returning to known facts, Ann Matthews moved into Boverton Place as a poor relation in 1722, at the age of nine. Elizabeth Seys, daughter of Wenllian and Richard Seys (IV), and her much older husband Evan were in possession of Boverton Place well before Ann's marriage.

We can now see that Iolo was right, in a way, to say that his mother's aunt was the "sister" of Ann Seys, later Lady King. Ann Seys was the great-granddaughter of Richard and Mary Seys, through their second son Evan; Wenllian's husband Richard was the grandson of Richard and Mary through their third son, Richard. Wenllian was therefore a generation above Ann in the Seys family tree but it seems likely that they were not far apart in age, and quite possibly would have addressed each other as "sister" after the fashion of the time.

Evan died in, or just before, 1733 (anon., 1863b) and Elizabeth remarried – but, under the terms of Evan's will, she would still have been the mistress of the household. Boverton Place may have been Ann Mathew's home until she married in 1744, when she was thirty-one, 22 years after she moved there. However, there is a possibility that she moved to another household before her marriage, which will be discussed later.

Elsewhere, Iolo gives more information (Williams, 1975, p.93), noting that his mother had been educated by her aunt in medicine, including some element of surgery, and that the two women provided medical treatment for those who could not afford treatment from a professional doctor.

This aunt would have been Wenllian. Perhaps her third husband, Thomas Rice of Cardiff, had died and she had returned to Boverton; according to the 1863 pedigree, she was buried in Llantwit Major, not in Cardiff. It was this relationship which first brought

Iolo's parents together. When Edward Williams sustained a severe injury to his hand, it was Ann's medical treatment that saved it from amputation and restored its function (Williams, 1975, p.93). They were married, Iolo says, "in about a twelve month" after their first meeting. Thus, they first met in 1743, when Ann was thirty years old, a late age for marriage in this period (Day, 2013, p.82). The marriage was held in St. Athan church on 8 November 1744 (Williams, 1975, p.81). The rector at the time was the "aristocratic" Charles Carne, who had been appointed in 1742; he had previously been the rector of the parish of Llanmaes, which contained Boverton (anon., n.d.b), so it is likely that he and Ann knew one another. Llanmaes, as will be seen, would witness a significant event for Iolo.

With this context established, we can move on to discuss why Mary Nicholl of Remenham, an Irish aristocrat, was willing to assist Iolo Morganwg, a poor stonemason from Glamorgan.

6. The Nicholls

The Hon. Mary Flower married the Reverend John Nicholl, the Rector of Remenham, on 8 January 1788 (Debrett, 1823, p.1131). She was 39 years old: very old for the time, when the average age of marriage was in the mid-twenties (Outhwaite, 1973, p.61). She would have been glad to marry; the Georgian age was cruel to spinsters, and an older unmarried woman ran the risk of being "brutally satirised" (Vickery, 2013, p.862). As we have already seen, with her brother having married and had an heir, Mary would not have owned any property, and so she would not have been seen as a particularly desirable match for suitors of her own social level, especially once she had passed her mid-twenties.

Her new husband's living of Remenham was no minor country parish: it was a prosperous town on the Thames, with some important aristocratic estates nearby. As previously noted, the main residence of the Flower family in Britain at this time was Old Windsor – a village very close to Remenham – so it is highly likely that they met here. During the eighteenth century, ecclesiastical posts were frequently not filled by the

Church itself; clergymen were appointed to these positions by those who had bought the right to do so. Often these were members of the local aristocracy or gentry, but for some – including Remenham – it was institutions. In fact, the right to appoint the Rector of Remenham had been purchased by Jesus College, Oxford in 1691 (Darwall-Smith, 2021). Jesus College had been established specifically for the education of Welsh students, and the Rector of Remenham was, as a result, usually a Welshman (Remenham Parish, n.d.).

John Nicholl (the family name is also 'Nichol', depending on the source; as with Mathew/Matthew/Mathews, contemporary spelling of names was inconsistent) was an alumnus of Cowbridge Grammar School (Hopkin-James, 1922, p.259). Dr Robin Darwall-Smith, archivist of Jesus College, Oxford, has kindly provided me with information about John Nicholl's subsequent academic and ecclesiastical career. He entered Jesus College on 24 November 1764, at the age of twenty. He was awarded his BA in 1768, and an MA in 1771. In the same year, he was made a Fellow of the College – a member of its governing body – which provided a small income. He took another degree while he was a fellow; this time a B.D. He obviously had financial resources: a degree was not cheap, and his family would have had to pay a third set of fees (Darwall-Smith, 2021).

The college had purchased the right to appoint the livings of a number of parishes, and it was usual that fellows would eventually take up one of these paid posts and resign their fellowship. This was to mutual advantage; the individual would move on to what was usually a substantially larger income, while the college kept the pool of its fellows fresh. The

Rectorship of Remenham was a good opportunity, so, when it became available in 1782, John Nicholl took it – suggesting that he was one of the more senior fellows. He resigned his fellowship in 1783, having settled in to his new position, and remained in the post until 20 February 1798 (ibid.).

When he married the Hon. Mary Flower, the Reverend John Nicholl was forty-one years old, having been born on 3 June 1746 (Burke, 1900, p.1172). He was therefore only a year older than Iolo Morganwg. This is important because John Nicholl's father was Whitlock Nicholl of the Ham.

Ham Manor lies just outside Llantwit Major, on a site that was once a residence of the lords of Glamorgan (Evans, 1943, p.204), both Welsh and Norman. The manor house itself was demolished after the Second World War (Kelly, 1971, p.50), and today the grounds house a retirement village of cabins (Berkeleyparks, n.d.). However, in 1722 – when Ann Matthews moved into Boverton Place to be with her aunt – Ham Manor was the home of Illtyd Nicholl, Rector of Llanmaes, until his death in 1733. The Reverend Nicholl had been born in 1673 (Burke, 1900, p.1171), so was 49 years old at the time. He would have been one of the Seys family's nearest neighbours: Ham Manor was approximately one mile from Boverton Place, so it would only have been a few minutes' ride by pony and trap, or a short walk away. The families would have seen each other regularly at social events in Llantwit Major, Cowbridge, and elsewhere.

The Nicholls were rising to become the social equals of the Seys at this time, and owned substantial amounts of land in Glamorgan and Monmouthshire. The family were originally Normans of Scandinavian origin, and had settled in Glamorgan in the late thirteenth century (Kelly, 1971, p.47). They had been at the Ham since 1597, when the manor's owner, Cecil (this was a female name in this period), heiress of the local branch of the Turbervilles, descendants of one of Fitzhamon's knights, married another Illtyd Nicholl, whose family had been in Llantwit Major for at least a century before that (James, 1975, p.212), living in Ty Mawr (Great House) on the town's outskirts (Gibbs, 1971, p.27).

The Illtyd Nichol living at the Ham in 1722 had married Susanna Whitlock, heiress of a family with properties in Devon and Somerset. They had four children: Whitlock (born in September 1720), Mary, (April 1721), Iltutus (January 1723), and John (who is recorded as dying in February 1773 at the age of 47, so was born in 1726) (Burke, 1900, pp.1171-2).

Illtyd Nicholl's children were all a few years younger than Ann Matthews, but close enough in age to have got on well with her. Whitlock, Illtyd's heir, was appointed Sheriff of Glamorgan for the year of 1746 (Nicholas, 1874, p.144). He was only 25 years old; the significance of this will be discussed later.

Whitlock married Anne Lewis of Penllyne in 1741, and they had fourteen children, of whom twelve lived beyond infancy: the oldest, Illtyd, was born in 1743 and the youngest, Mary, in 1767. John (1746) was the second child; the third, also Whitlock, was born in 1747, the same year as Iolo, and the fourth, Edward, in either 1749 or 1750. John Nicholl of Remenham and his brothers were therefore all childhood contemporaries of Iolo Morganwg.

John and Mary Nicholl of Remenham had no children of their own. However, theirs was not a childless household. As the first son, John's elder brother Illtyd should have been the heir of the Ham. Illtyd, like John, had been a Fellow of Jesus College and, like John, had moved on to become a parish rector – in his case, of Tredington in Worcestershire (Thomas, 1965, p.159), to which he was appointed in 1777 (anon., n.d.d). Illtyd and his wife Anne had had five children: two sons, and three daughters (Burke, 1900, p.1172). However, when Illtyd died suddenly in October 1787, his father, then aged 67, was still alive. The next in line to inherit then became Illtyd's oldest son, also called Illtyd.

Whitlock did not long survive his son, dying on 21 January 1788 (ibid.). However, as Evan Seys had provided for his widow Elizabeth at Boverton Place, and as Charles Edwin had provided for Lady Charlotte at Llanmihangel, Whitlock's will provided that his widow, Anne, should be able to enjoy his estate, and live in the Ham, until her death. In the end, she lived until January 1797, dying at the age of 75. The National Library of Wales has a paper from Iolo's collection, (Iolo Morganwg and Taliesin ab Iolo manuscripts and papers 7), which is a transcription of Anne's tombstone, so possibly Iolo himself carved the stone.

Whitlock's provision for his own widow meant that Illtyd's widow, Anne, was not able to access the estate's resources for ten years. Without them, she did not have the money to raise her children, so they were sent to relatives to be brought up, just as Ann Matthews had been. The eldest, the heir apparent Illtyd, went to London. The second son, Whitlock, was sent to be raised by John and Mary Nicholl in Remenham. At the time, he was three years old (Thomas, 1965, pp.159–160).

John and Mary schooled Whitlock themselves. They frequently spoke French to each other, and eventually engaged a Frenchman to tutor Whitlock in the language. Mary was also in the habit of visiting the needy residents of her husband's parish and would often be accompanied by the boy. In 1797, his brother Illtyd joined the household, after suffering from ill health in London (ibid.).

As we have seen, John Nicholl resigned from his post in Remenham on 20 February 1798, a year after his mother's death. He, Mary, and the two boys then retired to live "in Cowbridge", where Augusta, the boys' middle sister also lived (ibid.). It is possible that they joined Anne Nicholl and her children in the Ham itself, since it was described by the Nicholls themselves as being in Cowbridge despite being six miles away (Williams ab Ithel, 1862, p.viii).

Mary Nicholl, née Flower, died in August 1809 (Debrett, 1823, p.1131). John lived longer, dying on 16 July 1830 (Burke, 1900, p.1172). He was buried in Cowbridge on 3 August; his obituary described him as being "greatly respected and beloved" (anon., 1830). It is probable that Mary was also buried in Cowbridge. Above the north door of Holy Cross Church in the town are several memorial plaques relating to members of the Nicholl family. One refers to John's brother William (1751–1828; the plaque notes that he was "during many years Mayor of this Town"). His wife Frances (died 1819) was the daughter of the leading eighteenth-century physician and medical writer William Cadogan (Debrett, 1823, p.1131). The plaque says, "Their remains lie deposited in the same grave in the south-eastern part of the Church Yard of this Parish". An adjacent plaque names John's sister, Susanna (1760-1799), who had married a local man, John Bevan. The graves in the churchyard, like the plaques on the wall inside the church, tend to be grouped by family. This means that if John and Mary Nicholl were buried at Cowbridge, it would probably have been in the south-eastern part of the graveyard. Unfortunately, the graves cannot be identified today: many of the headstones in this part of the churchyard are now illegible, or have been removed.

There is another issue that needs to be considered about the relationship between Mary Nicholl and Iolo Morganwg, though. In one of his unsent letters to Mary Nicholl, written during their falling-out, Iolo resorts to what Charnell-White (2009, p.377) calls "sexual defamation". Responding to her accusation that he is a Jacobin, he calls her "a Lady-Jacobin" in return and adds a cryptic comment about the title of "Lady" being prostituted and used by "common strumpets". What reasons might he have had?

This question becomes particularly significant once we take a closer look at some dates. John Nicholl left Oxford and took up the living of Remenham in 1783. At the time, he was already thirty-seven years old and still unmarried. His elder brother, Illtyd, died in October 1787 and Whitlock, their father, died on 21 January 1788. John, now forty-one, had married the thirty-nine-year-old Mary Flower just a fortnight before, on 8 January 1788. Idealistic or romantic readers may take pleasure in the way that this middle-aged couple found each other just in time for John's father to give his blessing. The more sceptical might note that the marriage came at precisely the moment when John urgently needed a wife: he needed to establish a household which could be a home for his newly-orphaned nephew. Perhaps we may wonder whether this was simply a pragmatic marriage of convenience. John Nicholl, after all, was a younger brother with no property of his own. Remenham may have provided a good income for him, but he had come to it relatively late in life, so he did not have a great deal to offer to a potential bride. When he found it necessary to marry in a hurry, the field of candidates would not have been large. It would need to be someone like Mary Flower, who similarly had few options, and who would likely have jumped at a last, and unexpected, opportunity for marriage – and, if this is so, it might be an explanation for Iolo's calling her a "strumpet".

She may, perhaps, have had other reasons that are unknown to us. Her brother, William, had become the 2nd Viscount Ashbrook as a child and, as was mentioned earlier, married Elizabeth, the sister of one William Ridge, who came from Oxford (Burke & Burke, 1915, p.139). William died in 1780. Ten years later, in January 1790, Elizabeth remarried; her new husband was one Reverend John Jones DD (ibid.). The Clergy of the Church of England database lists only one John Jones with that qualification in that period (anon., n.d.c); he was appointed as the Vicar of Aberysgir in August of 1795. Aberysgir is only a few miles away from Abercynrig. John Jones' records show that he was appointed to the position by William, Viscount Ashbrook, whose office was in Ireland. This would have been the third Viscount, Elizabeth's son and Mary Nicholl's nephew, who was named after his father. It may simply be coincidence, but it is remarkable that two women of the Flower family, members of the Irish peerage, married Oxford-connected Welsh vicars within a short period of time.

In any case, this context makes it almost certain that when Mary Nicholl began to help Iolo Morganwg in 1791, it was at her husband's request. The Nicholls had not long been married, and Mary had probably had little opportunity to meet Iolo or learn much about him – and this explains why she would have been unaware of Iolo's politics.

This excursion through the history of the Nicholl family allows us to understand that after Ann Matthews' arrival in Boverton, Wenllian, her aunt, would have been preoccupied with the death of her husband and her subsequent remarriage, and probably left for some years to live in Cardiff. Although we know that Ann was educated at a boarding school, this would have been quite a lonely life. Whitlock Nicholl and his siblings were some years younger, but there can be no doubt that, living only a mile away, she must have spent a lot of time with them. Ann Matthews would have known Whitlock Nicholl well, from his childhood until his marriage in 1741. She may still have been at Boverton when his first child, Illtyd, was born in 1743.

This, however, brings us to a curious question. Williams (1956, p.92) notes that according to her marriage certificate, Ann Matthews was living in Llanmaes before her wedding, and wonders whether some of the Seys family had moved there. The Nicholl family, on the other hand, had very strong Llanmaes associations – Illtyd Nicholl had been the vicar there, as was the Charles Carne who conducted Ann's wedding. As we will see in the next chapter, Illtyd Nicholl's youngest son, John, lived in Llanmaes, and he would change Iolo Morganwg's life. Had Ann lived there for a period? It is not clear when Elizabeth Seys married her second husband, but this would have disrupted the household in Boverton. Is it possible that Ann was taken in by John Nicholl for a time? That might explain the later closeness of the Nicholl and Williams families.

In any case, after her marriage in 1744, Ann and her new husband lived in Llancarfan, seven miles away from the Ham, and once called "The Village of a Thousand Saints" (Emanuel, 1961, p.60). However, they soon moved to Flemingston, which would remain Iolo's main home for the rest of his life. Flemingston is only four and a half miles away from the Ham, so it must be assumed that Ann maintained contact with the Nicholl family; after all, she had known them as neighbours and social equals for over two decades while living in Boverton – and, possibly, Llanmaes. Iolo was of an age with John, Illtyd and Edward Nicholl, so he and John Nicholl would have known each other all their lives.

To John Nicholl of Remenham, Iolo was perhaps a childhood friend. At the very least, he would be a familiar local contemporary and the son of an old friend of John's parents. It would be entirely natural for him to help Iolo out, and this more than adequately explains why he and his wife used their networks to find subscribers for Iolo's volumes of poetry.

In fact, if we suppose that most of the subscribers to *Poems, Lyrical and Pastoral* who are explicitly linked to Oxford University were recruited by John (and adding members of the Nicholl family), then he actually raised more money (73 sets) for Iolo than his wife did. This is without counting the numerous clergymen who, like John Nicholl himself and his brother Illtyd, may well have been former fellows of Oxford colleges. Apart from the 73 sets sold to Oxford-linked clergy, a further 95 subscribers were clergymen or their family members, buying a total of 102 sets between them.

As we will see, one member of the Nicholl family would introduce Iolo Morganwg to one of his bardic teachers. Another, John Nicholl of Remenham, enabled him to publish his work. They were thus of huge significance to his life and works, and this can only be attributed to their having known his mother well. Without this connection with the gentry, and the Nicholls of the Ham in particular, we might never have heard of Iolo Morganwg.

However, we are not finished with the Nicholl family yet; they will reappear later in a previously untold aspect of Iolo's life and career, which will give us more to consider about John and Mary Nicholl.

7. A Bardic Introduction in Llanmaes: John Bradford

As we have seen, when Ann Matthews moved to Boverton, her neighbour at the Ham was Illtyd Nicholl. Illtyd's youngest son, John – Whitlock's younger brother, and the uncle of John Nicholl of Remenham – lived in nearby Llanmaes; his own son would become the Right Honourable Sir John Nicholl, MP for Merthyr Mawr (Burke, 1900, p.1172). This older John Nicholl would have a significant impact on Iolo's career; Williams (1956, p.120) records Iolo's recollection that the poet John Bradford was land-steward to John Nichols [sic] of Llanmaes, identified as the father of Sir John Nichols.

It is important to be wary of this statement. Few real facts are known about Bradford's life, and both Williams (1959a) and Lewis (2004a) emphasise the need for caution. After Bradford's death, Iolo claimed many of his literary forgeries were copies of manuscripts which he had been lent by Bradford; of course, Bradford could no longer be asked the truth of the matter. The same is true of John Nicholl of Llanmaes, who supposedly lent documents about Cowbridge Grammar School and other aspects of Glamorgan history to Iolo. As Davies (1967, p.339) observes, since John Nicholl of Llanmaes died in 1773 (Burke, 1900, p.1172), he would not have been able to repudiate any of Iolo's later claims.

However, there is no question about Iolo having been one of Bradford's students of poetry. This relationship is not disputed, so it is reasonable to ask how they met. It is one thing for Iolo to have claimed, after the death of both Nicholl and Bradford, that some of his material came from their documents. There was no way for anyone else to have verified this. It is quite another thing for him to have made the specific claim that Bradford worked for John Nicholl of Llanmaes as a land steward. That was a job which would have brought Bradford into contact with a very large number of people around the Nicholl family estates. In an agricultural community, memories are very long; quite apart from the other members of the Nicholl family, many of their tenant families, neighbouring gentry, local officials, merchants, and others would have known very well whether this was true or not. It is not something Iolo could have hoped to obfuscate or to go unremarked.

This being the case, there is reason to believe Iolo when he says that it was this John Nicholl who, on learning of Iolo's poetic ambitions, arranged the first meeting between the two. It may or may not have been true that it was during this meeting that Bradford bestowed upon Iolo a blue ribbon, "the insignia of the Primitive Order of Bards of the Island of Britain in [the] Chair [of] Glamorgan and Tir Iarll", but it is likely true that it was the Nicholl family who introduced him to one of his main mentors in poetry and in bardism.

Later biographers have attempted to present Bradford in more working-class terms, emphasising his work as a weaver, fuller, and dyer in Bettws (*Tir Iarll*) in the upland Glamorgan *blaenau* (Jarvis, 2009, p.49; Jenkins, 2009, p.273; Lewis, 2004a; Williams, 1959a), but it is likely that his relationship with Iolo originated through the gentry of the lowland Vale.

It may be worth noting here that Bradford did not do his weaving and dyeing himself; he owned a business in which other people did this work, leaving him time to pursue his literary interests (Williams, 1965, p.31). Perhaps it was his work for John Nicholl in the Vale of Glamorgan which enabled him to establish this business. Being a steward could be very profitable for the man concerned, and Jenkins (1983) notes that a number of families of the Glamorgan gentry owed their position to an ancestor who had exploited his role as an estate steward for personal advantage. Gibbs (1971, p.24) includes the Stradling and Carne families, who were later very influential, amongst the families who got their start in this way. To these, Martin (1979, p.19) adds the Edmondes family of Cowbridge, the Williams family of Duffryn, the Traherne family of Coedarhydyglyn (who will be discussed further later on), and even the Merthyr Mawr branch of the Nicholl family itself.

A steward had near-complete authority (Jenkins, 1984, p.43) over the land he managed. Rural estates in the eighteenth century still used a "charge-discharge" accounting system based on mediaeval practice in which estate owners could actually discover that they owed their steward significant sums of money at the end of the year – should the steward so manage the figures (Martin, 1979, pp.18-19; Baker and Eadsforth, 2011). It should be noted that the men hired to be stewards were often men of some substance themselves: members of gentry families which had fallen on hard times, younger sons who would not inherit, or the freeholders of small properties who needed an additional source of income (Martin, 1979, p.15). A steward would also need to have funds. Although the role was paid a salary and travelling expenses, a prospective agent needed to supply his employer with a bond as security against the monies he would be responsible for. Furthermore, an agent who did not have social status based on his own estate could not expect to be respected by his employer's tenants (ibid., p.17). Bradford fits the bill: his family had once had a higher social status, sufficient for them to have their own coat of arms, and he may well have inherited funds from his father, who had also been a dyer and fuller (Lewis, 2004a). That Bradford was *someone's* steward is supported by Jenkins (1979, p.44). The National Library of Wales holds a number of account books and correspondence of the Nicholl family, so further research may confirm their employment of Bradford.

8. The Prince of Wales

Possibly through Mary Nicholl's efforts of 1791, Iolo had been allowed to dedicate *Poems, Lyrical and Pastoral* to George Augustus Frederick, the Prince of Wales, but as we have seen, Iolo's anti-monarchism led to their falling out at the end of that year. The books were published in 1794, over two years later, when Nicholl angrily wrote once more to Iolo to denounce his republicanism (Constantine, 2009, p.139). This indicates that she and Iolo were still in contact at that time.

The year after that, though, Iolo was once again given permission to dedicate a poem to the prince. This was to celebrate the prince's wedding on 8 April 1795, and Iolo was permitted to deliver it to the prince in person at the prince's official home, Carlton House, in the fashionable centre of London. He was expecting a generous reward of around fifty guineas. In the event, he received only two (Jenkins, 2012, p.120).

This was a disaster. A pound was worth twenty shillings; a guinea was worth twenty-one. A shilling in turn was worth twelve pence. Iolo at around this time estimated that he could have a comfortable life with three shillings and sixpence a day (Jenkins, 1975, p.18), while a report from 1797 describes how a labouring family could pay for a year's rent and necessities for only five pounds and four shillings per family member (Twiston Davies & Edwards, 1939, p.41). Fifty guineas would have given him a year's income or more with which to resume his business efforts, pay off debts, and/or buy some land. It would essentially have given him the means to climb back into the ranks of the gentry. Now, his hopes were essentially finished.

Why was the prince's gift so derisively small? Was it because of Iolo's political views? The narrative followed in recent biographies assumes that it was. However, this requires us to believe that the Prince of Wales gave Iolo permission to dedicate *Poems* to him, was offended by their republican content upon their publication (or perhaps before, tipped off by Mary Nicholl) but then subsequently gave Iolo permission to dedicate a second publication to him, further gave permission for Iolo to meet him in person, and then gave an insultingly small amount. It seems far too elaborate.

Furthermore, the dates do not match this interpretation. As previously mentioned, we know that Mary Nicholl fell out with Iolo at the very end of 1791, and it has been assumed that she must have won permission for him to dedicate *Poems* to the prince before this. However, at the time of their angry exchange of letters, the marriage of the Prince of Wales to Princess Caroline was not even on the horizon. It was not agreed until 1794, so this permission could not have included any reference to the marriage.

This means that consent for Iolo to write a marriage poem must have been sought and granted in a completely separate application from the dedication in *Poems*. It is not impossible that Iolo did this on his own, but it may be that Mary Nicholl had continued to work on his behalf. Possibly Mary simply swallowed her anger and continued to help Iolo for her husband's sake. Alternatively, the Welsh are known, to the point of stereotype, for having violently emotional arguments which are afterwards soon quite forgotten (Richards, 1994, pp.58–59). Mary, being Irish, may have had the same temperament; in which case the surviving letters may not accurately reflect a genuine, though tempestuous, friendship. This explanation, for reasons which will become clear, is unlikely.

Another possibility is that the later dedication, perhaps even both dedications, had in fact been arranged by someone else – and there is a clear candidate for who that might have been.

The king, George III, favoured the Tories. The Prince of Wales was firmly in the Whig camp and spent a lot of time drinking and gambling with leading Whig politicians such as Charles James Fox and the Irish MP and poet Richard Brinsley Butler Sheridan (Maynard Bridge, 1922, p.264). Iolo was, of course, well known to the Whig MP for Glamorgan, Thomas Wyndham, who was thus in a position to communicate with the prince. As we have seen, Wyndham also had his own links with the royal family through his Edwin family connections, and he might well have felt inclined to assist Iolo in return for his help during the 1789 election campaign. That he had a close connection with, and affection for, Iolo is demonstrated by the fact that it was Thomas Wyndham's daughter Caroline, Countess of Dunraven and Mount-Earl, who later paid for a memorial to be placed on Iolo's grave (Robertson Spencer, 1913, p.155).

Iolo's friend Elijah Waring (1850, p.114) did not believe that the prince had been offended by Iolo's criticism of monarchy, particularly as it had been in the abstract, and he was probably right. As Waring describes, the prince himself had been known to praise political radicals such as the debauched journalist and politician John Wilkes, if only to annoy his father the king (ibid.; Maynard Bridge, 1922, p.262). It must also be considered that in 1794 Iolo had been personally interrogated about his political views and writings by William Pitt the Younger, Henry Dundas, and William Wyndham Grenville (Jenkins, 2012, p.111) – in other words, by the Prime Minister of the Kingdom of Great Britain, the Home Secretary, and the Foreign Secretary, all at once. He had been released, as they had not found grounds to charge him, but he was still watched by government agents afterwards (Jones, 2010, p.97). These were dangerous times for radicals: the monarchy and the government of Britain were paranoid, and with good reason, given that less than two years had passed since the executions of Louis XVI and Marie Antoinette in France. In Britain, suspected radicals were being tried for sedition and even treason, and *habeas corpus* had been suspended. Iolo was free only because he was not deemed to be a danger by the authorities – yet we are asked to believe that the Prince of Wales did consider him to be a republican revolutionary but despite this allowed him into his presence simply to deliver a snub. This makes little sense.

What if Elijah Waring was correct, and the prince was not particularly concerned about Iolo's republican views? What other reason could there have been for the snub?

9. Mary Robinson

At this point, another woman needs to be introduced because Iolo's mother, Ann Mathew, was not the first girl to have been taken in at Boverton. There may have been another before her, and her family's story adds depth to our understanding of Ann Mathew, of Mary Nicholl, and of the social networks in which Iolo moved.

That girl was Elizabeth: grandmother of Mary Robinson who, born Mary Darby in Bristol in 1757, was ten years younger than Iolo Morganwg – and who grew up to be forever connected in history with the Prince of Wales.

Mary begins her memoirs (written between 1797 and 1800, although they were not published until well into the nineteenth century) with the tale of her great-grandmother Catherine, who she identifies as the daughter of Richard Seys of Boverton. Catherine, she says, was the sister of Ann, later Lady King. Catherine married, although Mary does not give the name of her husband. The couple had one child, a daughter they named Elizabeth. However, both parents died when Elizabeth was an infant, and so the child was taken in by Richard and his family to be raised at Boverton. As she grew up, she became skilled in herbal medicine and, increasingly, spent time with her godmother, Lady Tynte of Halswell in Somerset. There the two women provided medical care and medicines to the local population. Elizabeth was, Mary writes, "the village doctress".

This story needs to be taken with a large amount of salt, since there are many things that do not add up – the most important being, of course, that neither Richard Seys (III) nor (IV) had a daughter named Catherine. Richard Seys (II) *did* – but she did not have a daughter called Elizabeth. There were other Richards in the extended Seys family who married women called Catherine, but none of them lived at Boverton.

While there is one more generation involved in Mary's story than in Iolo's account, and the sequence of names does not properly match anything in the 1836 Seys pedigree, the parallels with Ann Mathew's story are obvious. Is the account true? If it is, there is a possible explanation if we accept that Mary's recollection had become confused – or, perhaps, that she had not been told the exact truth by her relatives. Even if it is not, it is still important for our discussion of Iolo, as we will see.

One question to consider is whether the Seys family of Boverton were in the habit of taking in those who had nowhere to go. There is evidence that they were: Jenkins (1983, p.250) describes how wealthy families in England would send awkward or embarrassing relatives to "obscurity" in Wales, and how one such individual, a member of the Verney family of Buckinghamshire, died in Boverton in 1707 whilst staying in the home of Richard Seys (III). If they took in strangers, an orphaned relative would surely have been welcomed, and not only Ann Mathew.

Halswell House in Somerset was indeed the seat of the Tynte family, and Jane, the wife of the second Baronet, was Welsh; in fact, she was the heiress of the Kemys, or Kemeys, family of Cefn Mably (halfway between Cardiff and Caerphilly) (Nicholas, 1872, p.645). Her father, Sir Charles Kemeys, had been the Member of Parliament for Monmouthshire from 1685 to 1687, and again from 1695 to 1698; in between, he was the Member for Monmouth borough from 1690 to 1695. He died in December 1702, while acting as Governor of Cardiff Castle (Williams, 1895, p.137) Although Lady Jane's date of birth is not recorded, she married in 1704 and had three sons and a daughter before her husband died in 1710. Given that the average age of marriage was around 25, we can approximate her date of birth to around 1680. The date of her death is also unclear. Griffiths (1959) puts it as 1747, but Williams (1895, p.137) gives the specific date of the 17 December 1758 (although this may instead refer to the widow of Charles' elder brother John). The Kemys family were powerful, extremely active in the politics of the day, and early adopters of the principles of agricultural improvement (Jenkins, 1983, p.52). Both the Seys and Kemys families were ultra-royalists before and during the Civil War (ibid., pp.101–124). In Ann Mathew's generation, Jane's son, Charles Kemys-Tynte (1710–1785), became the Tory candidate for Glamorgan in 1745 (ibid., pp.162–163), suffering a surprise defeat despite a very strong campaign with substantial support from different factions of the gentry (ibid., p.172). As we will see, the defeat made little difference to him.

The strongest possibility is that Mary Robinson was a descendant of Roger Seys, the disinherited eldest son of Richard and Mary Seys, who became the Vicar of Llangyfelach in 1663 (anon., 1863b). Roger married Cecil, the daughter of Rowland Morgan, who owned the estate of Gwern y Clepa, once the home of Ifor Hael (Morgan, 2011, p.127), the ruins of which Iolo would later visit with the Reverend Evan Evans, or Ieuan Brydydd Hir (ibid., p.128). Roger and Cecil had a daughter called Catherine, who married and had three children (anon., 1863b), but her husband's name is not given by the 1863 pedigree. This odd omission mirrors Mary's account: she also does not name her great-grandfather. This same Catherine was bequeathed the sum of £5 per annum by her cousin Margaret, the sister of Richard (III), when Margaret died unmarried in 1695, so there is a clear indication that there was still a warm relationship between the women of the two Seys branches.

If this is the Catherine who became Mary Robinson's great-grandmother, she married a man named Petit (Davenport, 2006, p.4). There is a discrepancy: the 1863 pedigree says that Catherine Seys had three children, while Mary says that her great-grandmother Catherine had only one child.

If Mary Robinson was descended from Roger Seys, then her great-grandmother was of the same generation as Richard Seys (III). Her grandmother, Elizabeth, would have been the same generation as Ann, Lady King, and Ann Matthews; her mother Hester, who married Nicholas Derby, the same generation as Iolo.

Since Roger Seys was the first of his generation, his descendants would be born some years earlier than their peers in other branches of the family, and if we also take into account that Ann Matthews married late and had Iolo at an age when other women of her generation were already becoming grandmothers then it is quite credible that Mary Robinson was only ten years younger than Iolo despite belonging to the next generation. The dates also mean that it is plausible that Jane Tynte of Halswell could have been godmother to Mary's grandmother Elizabeth.

This leaves the issue that in this scenario Catherine's father was Roger, not Richard (III). The Clergy of the Church of England database (anon., n.d.a) records Roger as dying of natural causes in 1677. In her memoirs, Mary states that her grandmother Elizabeth died in 1780; from other comments made in the text, she must have been born in or around 1700. By then, Roger Seys had been dead for 23 years, so Elizabeth could not have been brought up by her grandfather. However, as we have seen, Richard's sister thought well enough of Roger's daughter Catherine to leave her an annual income in her will. It is therefore highly likely that if Catherine and her husband had both died, their infant daughter would have been taken in at Boverton. Here she would have been raised with Ann. So, it was Elizabeth, Mary's grandmother, who had Richard Seys (III) as her "father" and Ann, later Lady King, as her "sister".

It seems that perhaps Mary Darby, later Robinson, was told a highly edited version of her family history. It is very easy to speculate what the reason might be: Roger had been disinherited and had brought up four children on a vicar's living. Any property he had would have gone to his only son, Richard. Catherine and her two younger sisters would, like Ann Matthews, have had very little appeal to potential suitors in the gentry. Let us consider that, like Ann, Catherine married beneath her. When she and her husband died, Richard Seys of Boverton took in Elizabeth in the same way that John and Mary Nicholl of Remenham later took in John's nephew Whitlock, while the other two children went to other relatives. For the Nicholls, it was a temporary arrangement; Whitlock's mother was still alive. In the case of Elizabeth Seys, however, both parents were dead, so it makes complete sense that Richard Seys would raise her as his own child. She would naturally regard him as her father in all meaningful ways.

As we have seen, Richard (III) died in 1714, his heir Evan in 1720. By then, Elizabeth Petit was approaching her majority and was perhaps already spending more time with her widowed godmother in Somerset than in Wales. She had probably left Boverton shortly before Ann Matthews arrived – but she must have known Evan and Elizabeth Seys, and Elizabeth's parents Richard and Wenllian; possibly she also knew the young Ann Matthews.

This Boverton connection is very significant to our story because her granddaughter, Mary Robinson, is better known to history as "Perdita". She was a famously beautiful young actress and protégée of both David Garrick, one of the most influential figures in theatre during the eighteenth century, and Georgiana, Duchess of Devonshire. In 1780 she scandalised society by, despite being married and a mother, becoming the first, and high-profile, mistress of the still underage Prince of Wales – the same Prince of Wales to whom Iolo later dedicated his poems (Byrne, 2004, pp.105–142; Davenport, 2006, pp.56–93).

(The prince was eighteen at the time; the legal age of majority was twenty-one).

The prince had already demonstrated a liking for older women: in the previous year, 1779, he had declared his love for Lady Mary Hamilton, a twenty-three-year-old governess in the royal household. Like Mary Robinson, she was famously attractive; for the painter Sir Joshua Reynolds, she was the ideal image of a beautiful woman. The two became friends but, although the prince continued to woo her, she did not respond romantically. She was, however, devastated when the prince abruptly sent her a letter revealing that he was transferring his attentions to Mary Robinson (Davenport, 2004, pp.58-60; Royal Collection Trust, n.d.). Lady Mary had a connection to Glamorgan: her father, Charles Hamilton, was cousin-german to Lady Charlotte Edwin (née Hamilton) of Llanmihangel.

Mary Robinson's nickname came from the Shakespearean role she was playing on stage when the prince was in the audience. He had already seen her at social events and become enamoured of her, but it seems to have been during her performance as "Perdita" in *The Winter's Tale* that he decided to drop Lady Mary Hamilton and pursue Mary Robinson instead. She did not yield at once to his advances (Byrne, 2004, pp.110–115) but, once she did – despairing of her husband's ongoing infidelities and giving up on her belief in being a good wife – she did so enthusiastically, and the ensuing relationship scandalised London society.

The scandals continued after he, in turn, dropped her for another woman. She waged a very public campaign through the newspapers to force him to honour very substantial financial commitments he had made to her. In the end, she was paid off to keep her quiet and to prevent her from publishing love letters that he had written to her; the affair was becoming a threat to the reputation of the monarchy, which had already been undermined by the loss of the American colonies.

Later in life, Mary Robinson transformed herself into a well-known poet, an essayist, and an early feminist. She was a close friend of Georgiana, the influential Duchess of Devonshire and, despite having been an acquaintance, and possibly a friend, of Marie Antoinette (Byrne, 2004, pp.173–4), she would support the French Revolution. She was a friend of radicals such as Anna Laetitia Barbauld, Samuel Taylor Coleridge, William Godwin, and Mary Wollstonecraft, as well as many other famous names of the day. These were the same circles that Iolo Morganwg moved in during his second sojourn in London, while he was trying to publish his poetry. Did they know each other?

It is very tempting to imagine Iolo and Mary meeting at a dinner party and discovering their shared Seys connection amongst the debates over the nature of God or on "Liberty". Unfortunately, it seems unlikely. Mary does not appear to have entered these circles until after Iolo had dejectedly left London in the summer of 1795: she did not meet Godwin until the beginning of 1796 (Byrne, 2004, p.342), for example, and Coleridge only in 1799 (Davenport, 2006, p.204).

Another possibility is that they may have known each other through their mutual links with Bristol. Mary was born there and was educated by the celebrated Hannah More (Byrne, 2004, pp.11–13; Davenport, 2006, pp.8–9) who was later one of Iolo's literary supporters (Constantine, 2009, pp.128–90).

However, there is a much more likely way they may have known of the relationship. Apart from her Seys ancestry, Mary Robinson had other Welsh connections. Her husband, Thomas Robinson, was the illegitimate son (the nephew, he initially told her) of Thomas Harris – a successful tailor who had bought the Tregunter estate in Talgarth, Brecknockshire. His brother Howell, a leading figure of the Welsh Calvinistic Methodists, had established the Trefeca Academy. The funding for the academy had come from Selina Hastings, the Countess of Huntingdon – who was a close collaborator of Lady Charlotte Edwin of Llanmihangel in promoting Methodism; the latter was mentioned for her work in the memoirs of both the countess and those of John Wesley (Jenkins, 1954, p.188). One of Lady Charlotte's Methodist appointees, Thomas Davies, who was given the rich living of Coity, was a close friend of Howell Harris, frequently preached at Trefeca, and was a witness of Harris's will (Brown, 1993, pp.72–73).

Robinson was a black sheep: a liar, philanderer, and wastrel – but Mary did not realise any of this until after the marriage. His father disapproved of his son and, initially, of the marriage. However, presented with it as a fait accompli, he accepted it, and when the couple first visited him, he was very taken with Mary – although the female members of his household very definitely were not (Byrne, 2004, pp.43–5; Davenport, 2006, pp.23–4).

Very quickly, the young couple were in difficulties. Living in London far beyond their means, they ran up debts and were soon being pursued by their creditors. Unable to pay, and with Mary very heavily pregnant, they fled to Talgarth. Harris was unsympathetic; so much so that he refused to allow Mary to give birth in his home. She was sent to his brother's Trefeca seminary, where she delivered her daughter (Davenport, 2006, p.29; Byrne, 2004, pp. 58–60).

The girl, Maria Elizabeth Robinson, was born on 18 October 1774. Some weeks later, the couple's creditors learned where they were, and they were again forced to flee, now with their new-born daughter. They went to Monmouth, where Mary's grandmother Elizabeth, who had been brought up in Boverton by Richard Seys (III), had her home.

Mary's account suggests that Elizabeth was well-connected and well-to-do, and they stayed with her for around a month. As mentioned earlier, the son of Elizabeth's godmother, Charles Kemys-Tynte, had stood for election as the Member of Parliament for Glamorgan in 1745, and had lost. That election had been held on 2 January; on 14 March, he was successfully elected as the Member of Parliament for Monmouth instead. That he could do this is not surprising; apart from their land in Somerset, the family's inheritance of the Cefn Mably estates meant that they owned "extensive estates in [the counties of] Glamorgan, Monmouth and Brecon" (Williams, 1895, p.137). Given that we are told Elizabeth had spent a great deal of time at Halswell, Charles would have known her well; this and her childhood with the Seys family would mean that she would have known most of the gentry of south and mid Wales. Charles did not stay long in Monmouth; he left his seat two years later, in 1747, to become the MP for Somerset, retaining the seat until 1774 (ibid.).

While Mary Robinson and her family were staying in Monmouth, their creditors caught up with them and Thomas was arrested for debt by the Sheriff of Monmouthshire. It happened, though, that the sheriff knew Elizabeth well and, for her sake, personally escorted Thomas, Mary, and their daughter to London to ensure that they arrived safely (Byrne, 2004, p.61).

The dates are a little vague, but this seems to have been early in 1775, and the Sheriff of Monmouthshire in that year was William Nicholl of Caerleon (Nicholas, 1872, p.763). Nicholas (ibid., p.637) lists an Illtyd Nicholl living at the Ham in Glamorgan in 1872 who had been a Justice of the Peace for Glamorgan and Monmouthshire, and who had been Sheriff of Monmouthshire in 1831; his family coat of arms is described and is identical to that of the William Nicholl of 1775. The Nicholl family owned property at Cwrt Bleddyn, which is four miles from Caerleon – so this William Nicholl, Sheriff of Monmouthshire in 1775, was without any doubt a member of the same Nicholl family that played such an important role in Iolo's life. The National Library of Wales holds pedigrees of the Nicholl family which may establish the exact relationship.

Mary Robinson's grandmother Elizabeth was older than Ann Matthews although, as we have seen, they were of the same generation. She is recorded as having married in Somerset in 1723, the year after Ann arrived in Boverton (Davenport, 2006, p.4); she would have been living, perhaps, with her godmother, Lady Jane Tynte. Having grown up in Boverton in the care of Richard Seys (III), she would have known the Nicholl family well, as Ann Matthews would do after her. The circumstances strongly indicate that Elizabeth Varinton, née Petit, grandmother to Mary Robinson and resident of Monmouth, would have known Iolo's mother, either personally or through their family connection.

This gives us a situation in which Mary Robinson, a descendant of the Seys family, was escorted to London in 1775 by a member of the Nicholl family, neighbours to the Seys, and a personal friend of Elizabeth, who had been raised in Boverton by Richard Seys (III). William Nicholl knew very well who Mary Robinson was and what her relationship to Iolo's family was. Both of them knew, or would have known of, Iolo Morganwg through their family networks. When Mary Robinson became the centre of scandal and a major public figure only five years later, the entire Nicholl family would have known the story of this journey to London.

Shortly after their arrival, Thomas Robinson was imprisoned until he paid his debts; he was sent to Fleet Prison on 3 May 1775 and remained there for fifteen months. As often happened at the time, Mary voluntarily went to live with him in the prison, taking their daughter with her. Mary used the time to publish a volume of poetry: her first publication (Byrne, 2004, pp.62– 63). Iolo had arrived in London in the late summer of 1773 and worked there for a year. He would remain in the south of England for another three years, during which he periodically returned to the metropolis (Jenkins, 2012, pp.31–2). They were thus there at the same time and it is not impossible that they were introduced, perhaps by William Nicholl. Perhaps Iolo visited her in prison.

Ultimately, though, it does not matter whether Iolo Morganwg and Mary Robinson ever met in person, or even whether they knew about each other. Other people knew about the connection, and this may have had unfortunate consequences for Iolo.

In this reading of events, once Iolo advertised his descent from "Richard Seys of Boverton" in the preface to *Poems, Lyrical and Pastoral*, the game was up for him. In her memoirs, Mary Robinson describes her own relationship with the Seys family with pride. It must be assumed that she had made no secret of it during her life, and especially during her time as the prince's lover. Certainly, when her enemies later attacked her in the press in 1780, she was depicted in caricature as wearing a Welsh hat (Davenport, 2004, p.92; Byrne, 2004, p.108). Of course, this may have been due to her husband's Welsh connections, but even if Mary had never mentioned Richard Seys before, there was one person who knew and who potentially had a reason to tell the prince. That, of course, was Mary Nicholl of Remenham, who was married into a family which knew all about the Seys family, and whose husband's relative had escorted Mary Robinson and her family from Monmouth to London. Given the apparent bitterness of her falling out with Iolo, we can easily imagine her dropping a few discreet words into the right ears at court.

When the Prince of Wales met Iolo Morganwg then, it may well be that he did not care about Iolo's political views. However, he had suffered considerable embarrassment and expense over Mary Robinson, and he may have decided that he was not going to give more money to her uppity poor relation. This provides one alternative, and much simpler, explanation for the snub, and for the snuffing out of Iolo's financial hopes and social aspirations. Even so, it does not explain why the prince would have given permission for the Iolo to write a wedding poem. If the connection with "Perdita" and the Seys family was enough to damn Iolo, then that second permission would not have been granted. There is a third, and more likely, possible reason, though, which will be discussed later.

There are other insights to be gained from Mary Robinson's story.

It is clear from her memoirs that "society" in the London of the 1770s and 1780s was one of frequently relaxed morality. The shift of large numbers of people from the countryside to the city, combined with widespread literacy and a rise in affluence amongst the middle and upper classes led to a new focus on personal independence and fulfilment, encouraged by a new "depravity" in the press (Roberts et al., 2004, pp.27–31). "Genteel society" was riddled with aristocratic rakes and libertines seeking to seduce an attractive woman be she married or not, and it was commonplace for a wealthy man to maintain a mistress; both Byrne (2004) and Davenport (2006) make this abundantly clear in their biographies of Mary Robinson, as does Foreman in her biography of Mary's friend and patron, Georgiana, the Duchess of Devonshire (1998). Before the Hon. Mary Flower married the Rev. John Nicholl, she and her sister Elizabeth seem to have been living in London (at least, that is where Elizabeth was living at her death, and it seems reasonable to assume that Mary had lived there during her single days). As we have seen, it seems likely that neither of them had much money or was seen as a great prize for marriage. As already noted, when Mary married John Nicholl in 1788, she was thirty-nine years old. It may be reasonable to wonder whether Iolo was aware of some gossip about her life and relationships in her unmarried years. Perhaps this is why Iolo sourly referred to her as a "common strumpet", and to the prostitution of the title of "Lady"?

Might Mary Robinson and Mary Flower even have known each other in London? In her unmarried days, Mary Flower was an aristocrat and moved in aristocratic circles, as the list of subscribers she recruited for Iolo shows. So, too, did Mary Robinson, through her association with the Prince of Wales and his circle, and her friendship with the Duchess of Devonshire. It is an intriguing possibility. She definitely knew the Nicholl family and seems to have been on good terms with them. She was proud of her Seys roots in Glamorgan. Her grandmother lived in Monmouth, which was a staging point for the coaches between London and Brecon (Scott Archer, 1970, p.26), and her father-in-law lived in Talgarth, close to the Flowers in Abercynrig. Members of the Flower family travelling between Old Windsor and Abercynrig would therefore have had to pass through Monmouth and would quite likely have broken their journey there; as we have seen, Mary Robinson's grandmother was socially well-connected. It cannot be proven, but there are good odds that they did know each other. Given that they also knew the Nicholl family, we have another link to Iolo.

Separately, Iolo's preface to *Poems* was written very shortly before its publication. Its style and his depiction of his mother and his youth are uncannily similar to Mary Robinson's description of her own mother and childhood. Both emphasise the goodness of their mother; both paint a picture of themselves as a talented child who shrank from the company of other children, preferring to spend all their time with their mother. As Byrne (2004, p.66) explains, this was a style of writing which became common in the 1790s, influenced by the gothic and sentimental literature of the time (ibid., p.11). Although Iolo was writing a few years earlier than Mary, who began her memoirs in January 1798 (Davenport, 2006, p.1), they were writing for the same audience. This lends support to Jenkins' suggestion that the picture Iolo painted of his mother was highly stylised (2012, p.11). Later, we will have reason to reconsider Ann Matthews' role as a mother.

10. Williams, Walters, and Malkin

As we saw in previous chapters, it seems unlikely that the Prince of Wales gave Iolo such a minimal gratuity for his poetic tributes because of Iolo's political views. It is possible that it might have been because of Iolo's family connection with Mary Robinson, but as we have seen, there are also problems with that explanation. However, there is a third possible reason which is even more probable, and this is to be found in the writings of Benjamin Heath Malkin.

Malkin was born in London in 1770 and trained to become a lawyer, qualifying in 1791. He was a cockney, having been born within earshot of the bells of St Mary-le-Bow church, but he had very strong Glamorgan connections since, in or around 1794, he married Charlotte, who was the daughter of the Reverend Thomas Williams, headmaster of Cowbridge Grammar School between 1764 and 1783 (Murphy, 2004).

The school had been founded in the early 1600s by the Stradling family of St Donats (Davies, 1967, pp.12–15). One of its pupils some decades later was a farmer's son, Llywelyn ap Siencyn of Llantrisant, who would walk to the school barefoot in all weathers, and who never forgot his early lack of money. At the end of his life, he had money aplenty because Llywelyn, remembered by the Anglicised form of his name, Leoline Jenkins, prospered. He entered Jesus College, Oxford (the Welsh college) as a "servitor": a student who would fund his education by working for the college. The Civil War interrupted his studies: as a royalist, he followed the future King Charles II into exile in France. This loyalty led to him becoming a fellow of the college upon the Restoration even though he had not yet completed his degree. His career took him to the heights of Royal service: knighthood, ambassador, Judge of the Admiralty Court, privy councillor, and secretary of state (ibid., p.21).

After retiring, Jenkins set about organising his legacy. He bought the grammar school from the Stradling family and, in his will, bequeathed it to Jesus College – more specifically, to "the Principal, Fellows, and Scholars" of the college (ibid., pp.22–23). This set up a relationship which endured for centuries, in which alumni of the grammar school proceeded to Jesus College for their higher education and, importantly for our narrative, the principal of Jesus College appointed the master of the grammar school (no doubt having first sounded out the feelings of the college fellows). In his will, Jenkins also provided bursaries for a number of pupils each year who could not otherwise have attended the school.

From 1768 to 1802, the Principal of Jesus College was Joseph Hoare. Originally from Cardiff, he had attended Cowbridge School himself before going on to Jesus

College, where he obtained his BA in 1730 and his MA in 1733. This was not enough for him, it appears, as he went on to obtain a BD in 1741 and a DD in 1768 (anon., 2020). At the time that Hoare became principal, the master of Cowbridge School was Thomas Williams, a local man, who had been appointed in 1764. Like Hoare, Williams had attended Jesus College, where he had obtained a BA (1752) and a BD (1763); he was a fellow from 1758 to 1765 (Davies, 1967, p.147). From 1759, he had been the Vicar of St Donats, and also held other livings. This meant that he was receiving salaries for several ecclesiastical jobs – although he did not generally do the work, leaving that to poorly paid local curates. As a result, he became affluent, making his two daughters, Charlotte and Elizabeth, very eligible (ibid., p.56).

Thomas Williams died in office in 1783. His successor as master was the Reverend John Walters, the oldest son of John Walters, curate of Llandough, who had been one of Iolo's early tutors in Welsh grammar, and who had involved him in collecting material for one of the first Welsh dictionaries. He resigned the following year to become the master of the school in Ruthin, where he died young of tuberculosis. He was followed by his younger brother, the Reverend Daniel Walters, who ran the school from 1784 to 1787 (ibid., pp.63–65).

John and Daniel were both former students of Cowbridge School. John had gone on to Jesus College in 1778. He had excelled, becoming one of the college's scholars in 1780, and then a sub-librarian of the Bodleian Library. A talented poet in both Welsh and English, he was also to become a fellow; his time at Oxford overlapped with the period when John Nicholl was also there as a fellow, having not yet moved to

Remenham. Daniel, unlike his brother, had not gone to Oxford; he went straight to work as a teacher at the grammar school in Norwich. Like his elder brother, he was a talented poet. Nevertheless, when John was appointed as master of Cowbridge School, Daniel also returned to Wales; he was given the living of Talygarn, near Pontyclun (ibid.). This mediaeval church has, according to the Database of Anglican Clergy, the distinction of being the only "private chapel" in the Diocese of Llandaff and had been restored using funds left in Leoline Jenkins' will (ancientmonuments. uk, n.d.). The living was in the gift of Jesus College, so Daniel was appointed by Joseph Hoare (Davies, 1967, p.63) despite never having been one of the college's students. Clearly, the Walters family was held in high esteem by Hoare and the fellows of Jesus College.

The Walters brothers had been very close to Iolo since the late 1770s, particularly Daniel, to whom he became a "boon companion" (Davies, 1967, p.379). He and Iolo spent a great deal of time together despite the difference in age. Both brothers were strong supporters of his poetic efforts and took his theories on Welsh history very seriously (Jenkins, 2012, pp.53–54). Thus, we know that Iolo was very close to the elder John Walters, and to at least two of his three sons. As Rector of Llandough, which is a short and easy walk from Cowbridge, Walters must have known his fellow ecclesiastical Thomas Williams, and so would his sons, particularly John. A further reason to believe this is the shared connection with Jesus College, Joseph Hoare, and the community of past and current fellows.

Since Iolo Morganwg was so close to the Walters family, it cannot be doubted that he also knew the

Williams family as part of the same social network – and he would therefore have known Williams' daughters, Charlotte and Elizabeth, as they grew up. Thus, when Charlotte married Benjamin Heath Malkin, Iolo would already have known her for many years.

Malkin, as noted above, was a Londoner, and a lawyer. He had attended Cambridge University, not Oxford. How did he come to meet Charlotte, resident of Cowbridge, in the first place? If they married in 1794 then, allowing for initial acquaintance and courting, they would have met perhaps a year or two beforehand, around 1791 or 1792. Curiously, this is the time when Iolo Morganwg of Cowbridge arrived in London with the support of the Nicholls of Remenham, seeking to publish *Poems, Lyrical and Pastoral*. Is it possible that Iolo in some way introduced Malkin to his future wife? The dates and social networks certainly fit. Even if not, at the time of their marriage Iolo already knew Charlotte, meaning that his connection with Malkin was a long one, likely dating from the late 1780s or early 1790s, rather than a brief and superficial one as suggested by Löffler (2007, pp.12–13) or Suggett (2009, p.207).

Malkin, at the time of his marriage, had recently qualified as a lawyer and lived in London until moving to Bury St Edmunds in 1809 to become the headmaster of the grammar school there. He and Iolo moved in similar radical circles, and Malkin also became an early supporter of the engraver and mystical poet William Blake. The Malkins' first child died in 1802, aged six. The boy – Thomas, presumably named for Charlotte's father – had been extremely talented, and the grief-stricken father published a book recording his achievements. Malkin employed Blake to design the book's frontispiece and the book was eventually published in 1806, although the actual engraving had been done by someone else. In his introduction to the book, Malkin included an account of Blake's life to that point, so clearly, he was already well acquainted with Blake.

Previous biographers, for example Mee (2009, pp.173–198), have been uncertain about the extent to which Iolo Morganwg and William Blake knew each other, or if they ever actually met in person. It has been judged possible, given their shared connection with the radical publisher Joseph Johnson. Johnson had intervened to ensure that Iolo's volumes of poetry were published, and he both employed Blake as an engraver and published his books (ibid., pp.175–6). However, the fact that Malkin was very friendly with both men, and that all three were in London at the same time in the mid-1790s, is a very strong indication that they would indeed have met.

The Malkins evidently maintained and valued their connection with Cowbridge, as they moved there in 1830 (the year of John Nicholl's death) to live in the Old Hall on the town's High Street (Hopkin-James, 1922, p.160). Malkin had recently retired after nearly twenty years as headmaster of the Bury St Edmunds grammar school. Perhaps on their previous visits he and Charlotte had known Henry (1766–829), the third son of John Walters of Llandough. Henry also attended Cowbridge School (Davies, 1967, p.61) but, unlike his brothers, does not seem to have been a poet and did not enter the Church. Instead, he took over the printing business of Rhys Thomas, who had set up the first press in Cowbridge, and who had printed many volumes of John Walters' English-Welsh dictionary (compiled with help from Iolo Morganwg) as well as one of Iolo's own early publications in Welsh, before succumbing to financial distress. Henry Walters was not an active businessman and sold the business in 1791 (Davies, 1959). Over the years, he became more and more eccentric, reclusive, and impoverished, living in increasing squalor in a house full of books and manuscripts opposite the Bear Hotel on Cowbridge High Street, and just a couple of buildings away from Old Hall. He would sometimes admit visitors, who wrote with awe of the scope of his erudition and eloquence. It is pleasing to imagine him being visited by Iolo Morganwg and to wonder at the conversations they might have had.

Benjamin Heath Malkin died in Cowbridge in 1842 and was buried there. A commemorative plaque on the wall in Holy Cross Church, close to the altar, marks the dates of birth and death of both Benjamin and Charlotte; it records her as being born on 2 January 1772 and dying in Cowbridge on 19 April 1859. Curiously, his details have been partially obscured, while hers have at some point been freshly marked to make them more legible.

A nearby plaque mentions Charlotte's sister Elizabeth. On 14 January 1793, she married William Williams of Dolgellau; it was his twenty-eighth birthday (Davies, 1967, p.65). William also went on to become the master of Cowbridge School for an almost unbelievable sixty years, from 1787 to 1847. He took over from Daniel Walters who, like his brother John, had died tragically young as a result of tuberculosis. Williams was also a graduate of Jesus College, and a protégé of both Joseph Hoare and the Bishop of Llandaff (ibid.), further indicating the close-knit nature of this group.

Returning to the Prince of Wales and his slighting of Iolo, we have established that Malkin knew Iolo well, and over many years, through being a part of Cowbridge society. Through his association with Cowbridge he had become one of Iolo's close friends and, ultimately, "one of his greatest admirers" (Jenkins, 2012, p.203). In the year after publishing his son's biography, Malkin published a two-volume guide to south Wales, *The Scenery, Antiquities, and Biography, of South Wales*, in which he dedicated several pages to a character portrait of his old friend Edward Williams: Iolo Morganwg (Malkin, 1807, pp.195–201). He notes Iolo's stubborn character and describes how it led him to never go back on a resolution: even if he came to realise that one was counterproductive, he would not break the promise he had made to himself. He writes (p.198, emphasis added):

"[H]e had in early life a habit of making resolutions, **which he has never broken in a single instance**, though in many cases he has lamented their inconvenience or absurdity."

One such resolution was that he would never read his own poetry aloud, a resolution dating back to his youth:

"In early life he was frequently invited by the gentlemen of the county, who took a pleasure in hearing him recite his poetry: but he conceived himself to be treated with less respect than other guests and made a resolution never again to repeat his own verses." (ibid., p.199)

As a result, Malkin writes, **"[h]e has often offended those, who were disposed to be his patron, by the refusal"** (emphasis added).

There is no doubt that Iolo was as stiff-necked as Malkin describes him. It is therefore only too easy to imagine him arriving at Carlton House to deliver his praise-poem for the Prince of Wales' marriage, being asked to read it aloud... and refusing to do so.

One can imagine the reaction of the prince and his court. Their day had already put them in a bad humour: the prince intensely disliked his new wife, and the wedding brought no joy to him or his circle. Although he is recorded by Lord Malmesbury as being "very civil and gracious" after the ceremony, the prince "had manifestly had recourse to wine or spirits" (Maynard Bridge, 1922, p.274). Now here was a lowly Welsh mason who had been given a great honour: the privilege of being allowed to dedicate not only two volumes of poetry but also a wedding poem to the prince. All he needed to do to earn a substantial gratuity was to read his poem aloud – but this republican relative of the troublesome Mary Robinson stood there in the prince's own home and said "no". What would be more likely than to throw him a trifling amount for his efforts and dismiss him?

After this humiliation, and the failure of Iolo's efforts to build a lasting career as a poet in English, he returned home to Glamorgan: to his wife and family, and to the social networks in which he had grown up. We can now begin to put these into a larger context, beginning with his romantic career.

11. Kitty Deere and Margaret Roberts

As a young man, Iolo took quite an interest in the young women around him (Jenkins, 2012, p.17). One of them in particular was the educated daughter of a minor landowner, who had a talent for poetry and was an only child (who would therefore inherit everything).

She married someone else. Iolo later married another young woman with a talent for poetry who was also an heiress, a woman who could discuss philosophy and who was "lively, literate [and] intelligent" (Morgan, 1975, p.8).

Already in this story we have discussed men who held the office of sheriff, in both Glamorgan and Monmouthshire. Possibly taking their cue from Hollywood, many of Iolo's biographers have believed that this was a sign of high social rank, and this has been particularly influential in discussions of Iolo's early romantic interest in Kitty Deere, the daughter of Matthew Deere of Ash Hall, Ystradowen, who had been Sheriff of Glamorgan in 1743 (Nicholas, 1874, p.143).

Morgan (1975, p.8) grandly declares as fact that the difference in social rank would have made a relationship between the two impossible in the eighteenth, or even the nineteenth, century. Jenkins (2018, p.37) describes her as *y ferch fonheddig anghyraeddadwy* ("the unattainable noble girl") and unkindly suggests that she was no more than a "prick-teaser". Elsewhere, he proposes that the difference in social status between them made Iolo's romantic feelings socially unacceptable and unreciprocated (2012, p.27).

However, this does not reflect the realities of the role of a sheriff in the eighteenth century. During the Norman and mediaeval periods, the position of high sheriff had been an important role in the administration of the Lordship of Glamorgan (Altschul, 1971, pp.63–65). However, it is important to point out that unlike, say, the Sheriff of Nottingham, the Sheriffs of Glamorgan were never officers of the Crown – because Glamorgan was a Marcher territory. By Iolo Morganwg's time, that position had in any case long been replaced by the county sheriff, created by Henry VIII's *Statutum Walliae* of 1542 (Williams, 1919, p.160) in order to carry out the commands of the Justices of the Peace. The position had been declining in status ever since, with its powers being transferred to the shire's deputy lieutenant (Jones, 1984, p.76), and to the Justices of the Peace (ibid., p.80). Even today, it is no ceremonial title given to honour a grandee. It is a job with a purpose: "supporting the Crown and the judiciary" (Howell, n.d.). Since the twentieth century, the office has been referred to as the "High Sheriff", but in Iolo's time, it was not so dignified and was simply "the Sheriff" (Williams, 1966, p.38).

In the eighteenth century, when, as has been noted, there was no centralised state apparatus, the position of sheriff was a hands-on role of law enforcement. It came with a lot of powers and influence, but it was unpaid; in fact, it cost the office-holder a lot of money and demanded a great deal of time and effort. The sheriff, for example, was expected to pay for hosting and entertaining any dignitaries who visited the county, which also involved ensuring that he and his household were all dressed to look the part (Heal & Holmes, 1994, p.174). Trying to avoid these expenses was frowned upon and might have resulted in a costly response from the gentry network (ibid.). Depending on the ability of his staff, over which he might have little control, the sheriff also ran the risk of becoming entangled in expensive legal cases (ibid.). The county sheriff served at the Great Sessions and was also responsible for declaring the results of elections, and so was exposed to political factions which, as we have seen, could be violent and unscrupulous.

The reality was that appointees were chosen randomly from a list of three nominees per county by the Crown, for one year only, because few people either wanted to do it or could afford to do it (Shrievalty Association, n.d.; Williams, 1919, pp.77–78; Thomas, 1976, p.21). Rather than being an honour, it was regarded as an unwelcome burden (John, 1966, p.15). The list of candidates was prepared by the Justices of the Great Sessions (Williams, 1919, p.160), and it was often only those of lesser influence and status – the young (such as Whitlock Nicholl), minor gentry, or even ordinary farmers – who would be entered on that list (Jenkins, 1983, pp.92–93). Those with more influence would use it, and that of their network, to try to make sure their names were left off (Heal & Holmes, 1994, p.174). It was certainly the case that those who were chosen could be excused, and the role allocated to another candidate, if they paid a substantial fine. Many felt it worth their while to do so (John, 1966, p.15). Only on rare exceptions might someone actively seek out the office – for example, newcomers to a county or rising youngsters who wished to make their mark amongst the local community (Heal & Holmes, 1994, p.174).

Thus, for example, when John Nicholl of Remenham's father, Whitlock, took office as Sheriff of Glamorgan in 1746, it was reported that he was accompanied by a huge, and almost unprecedented, cavalcade of "respectable" supporters (John, 1966, p.70). It may be that this was a celebration – he was the first Nicholl to hold the office. Equally, it may have been a show of force, making it known that despite his youth he should not be trifled with, and that his family and their powerful friends were watching over him. Indeed, both could be true.

The Deeres of Ash Hall belonged to the lowest grade of the gentry (Jenkins, 1983, p.293). Like many of their contemporaries in the Glamorgan gentry in the second half of the eighteen century, they had risen to this status from their beginnings as estate stewards to older gentry families (Jenkins, 1979, p.43). Thus, Matthew Deere had not been the Sheriff of Glamorgan because he and his family were of a social grade far above Iolo; he had been sheriff because he was too lacking in influence to avoid being appointed and was unable or unwilling to pay the fine to be excused.

There has also been a misunderstanding about social class, driven by modern conceptions and not reflecting the different attitudes towards class in eighteenth-century Wales and England. It has been assumed because Edward Mathews had to sell his land, and because Ann Matthews therefore had to marry a stonemason, that she and her sons were thereby cast out from polite society; that Iolo was condemned from the time of his birth to be a member of the lower classes with an impenetrable social barrier above him.

This was not the case. It is true that, in England, differences in social status were more meaningful and more deeply entrenched; Iolo's own complaints about how he was treated by Mary Nicholl's contacts show us that. Wales was different, however, for several reasons.

First of all, in Wales, two different social systems still existed alongside each other, coexisting and gradually merging. Many of the gentry families of Glamorgan traced their ancestry to the native Welsh nobility, predating Fitzhamon's conquest. To them, membership of the gentry was as much about genealogy as it was about property, and a man of little wealth would still be regarded as a gentleman if his family tree made him one. Indeed, it was entirely normal in Wales at this time for a squire to be the first cousin of a ploughman – and they would both consider themselves gentlemen through descent (Jones, 1976, p.31). Jenkins (1983, p.17) notes how such Welsh-style gentry "were notorious for their pride", and this fits exactly with Elijah Waring's anecdote of Iolo firmly stating that he knew his pedigree for generations, with many of them being "men of rank, and wealth, and power" (Waring, 1850, p.137). Indeed, a Welsh pedigree was a "dark science", which "would soon sober any one [sic] who approached it in an inquiring fashion without some training and qualifications" (Bradley, 1909, p.267). The fact was, though, that in Glamorgan a Welsh pedigree could usually be traced back, however unreliably, to the Dark Ages or before, while English titles were relative newcomers, with no noble lines older than the Norman Conquest. The Welsh family trees therefore were respected, and desirable, for their antiquity (Jones, 1976, pp.29–30). Even as late as the early twentieth century, it could be said that "everybody who is anybody in Glamorgan traces his pedigree to one or all of five Welsh families of ancient Morgannwg" (Griffith, 1904, p.4). The two most prominent of these were the descendants of Ifor ap Morgan in the east, and those of Iestyn ap Gwrgant in the west (Smith, 1971, p.25).

Secondly, Ann Matthews' situation was far from unique. The gentry in Wales had at this time only relatively recently (since late Tudor times) adopted the system of "strict settlement" primogeniture (anon., 2008a; Jones, 1976, p.30) in which the eldest son inherited everything, although the older Welsh system of gavelkind was to continue for some time after that (Jones, 1984, p.66). Primogeniture meant that younger sons received little or nothing; many of them fell into poverty in exactly the same way as Ann Matthews, but this did not necessarily mean that they lost their status (Jones, 1976, pp.35–36). Jenkins (1983, p.28) makes this clear; different branches of a family would unite to defend the honour of a member who had fallen on hard times, even if they were in bitter dispute over other issues. As he notes, even if a member or branch of the Matthews family was reduced to working in domestic service, their powerful relatives would watch over them, and protect them where necessary. Ann Matthews was, of course, a member of this very family.

Thirdly – and this applies to Iolo – it was quite normal for gentlemen whose families had fallen into poverty to climb back up by succeeding as merchants, professionals such as doctors or lawyers, or members of the clergy; these same routes could also make a gentleman of someone of humble origins (Jenkins, 1983, p.35; Jones, 1976, p.35). Seen in this context, Iolo's business efforts of the 1780s should properly be understood as the efforts of a member of the gentry to regain his family's former status. There was no "glass ceiling" to prevent him.

Thus, as Williams (1956, p.133) recognises, Iolo was not turned down as a suitor for Kitty Deere because of social difference; in the context of the time, they would probably not have considered that much of a difference existed. He was turned down because she was an heiress, and heiresses were "great prizes" (anon., 2008) for gentlemen seeking to expand their family's holdings of land. Land, after all, meant rental income. Marriage amongst the gentry in the eighteenth century was rarely concerned with the romantic feelings of the individuals involved; it was normally a pragmatic match calculated to increase family wealth and status. With Kitty Deere being an heiress, her father would have been the one to choose her husband. It is entirely possible that Kitty did indeed have romantic feelings for Iolo but her father chose someone who was able to bring more to the table.

This leads us to another question that has surprisingly not been discussed before. Iolo later married Margaret (Peggy) Roberts – but why did the Roberts family accept him, when the Deeres did not?

Margaret was also an heiress: she was the only child of Rees Roberts who had lands worth £1,000 (Williams, 1956, p.415) – a substantial sum which was enough to qualify the owner as a member of the lesser gentry (Jenkins, 1983, p.50). Roberts was renting the land out for £1 per acre (Cadrawd, 1904, p.1), so he had a rental income. The difference between yeoman farmers and the gentry was precisely this: the former worked the land themselves; the latter rented it out to others and lived off the income (Rhys & Brynmor-Jones, 1923, p.449). The other distinguishing matter was the family pedigree (ibid.), but as we have seen, Iolo had this through his mother, and in any case there were other ways to enter the ranks of the gentry. Margaret Roberts was thus on, or not far from, the same social level as Kitty Deere, and should also have been a prize. As with Kitty Deere, by the custom of the day, it would have been her father who decided upon a husband for Peggy, and he would have been expected to make that choice based on the best financial interests of the family.

It was the case that Rees Roberts was heavily indebted, having taken out mortgages on the property (Jones, 2009, p.231; Morgan, 2011, p.129); Morgan (ibid.) also says that the property was subject to substantial fees for the upkeep of drainage channels and sea defences. Possibly this discouraged potential suitors – but although this would be an insuperable burden to Iolo, who had no capital, it would not necessarily have deterred a rising merchant, lawyer, or clergyman with money who wished to cement his status as a gentleman by acquiring land through marriage. It seems, though, that Iolo had no idea about any debts until after his marriage (Jenkins, 2012, pp.50–51), and if he did not know, they could not have been common knowledge – so this does not seem to be the likely reason.

Jenkins (2012, p.51) also describes how Iolo's solicitor, William Rees, having been entrusted with the documents for Margaret's inherited land, refused after three years to return them or to act any further on Iolo's behalf. Even understanding that the times were different, this seems extraordinary behaviour for a legal professional. This was, Jenkins says, "sometime in the late 1780s". Again, it is curious that this has not previously been questioned. Why would a solicitor behave in this manner, and why would Iolo have let it stand?

The answer to these questions may lie in a short article in the *Cardiff Times* in 1904.

According to Cadrawd, (1904, p.1) the Roberts family's title to their land was questionable. Morgan (2011, p.128) says that Rees Roberts' farm was inherited from his brother William, of whose substantial properties it was only a part. Cadrawd, however, tells a different story: it, and other farms in the area, had been let rent-free around 1690, on a 99-year lease, by Edward Mansell – the nemesis of Iolo's grandfather – in return for debts being paid down. As the decades passed, the tenants, since they were not paying rent, increasingly thought of the land as their own property. By the time the leases were approaching expiry, the Mansell male line had died out and the estate had been acquired by Thomas Mansel Talbot through marriage (Anon., 2008c). He, according to Cadrawd, served notice on the tenants, causing a panic. This would fit the timescale given by Jenkins and would explain why William Rees would not return the farm's documents to Iolo. Iolo was unable to pay the debts secured on the farm and so was eventually committed to the debtors' prison in Cardiff. The farm was put up for sale while he was imprisoned, in February 1787 (Morgan, 2011, p.131), but Peggy Williams only eventually managed to sell it in 1793 (Jenkins, 2009, p.135) while Iolo was in London, and even then for much less than its face value (ibid., p.370), so it may be that Talbot's attempt to reclaim the land was still being disputed.

Cadrawd's article also makes some assertions about Peggy Roberts herself, which might provide the most significant reason why she was not courted as widely as might be expected. Cadrawd asserts that Rees Roberts was Peggy's stepfather, not her biological father. Rather, she was the illegitimate child of a relationship her mother had had before her marriage. Cadrawd does not identify Peggy's actual father but suggests that his name was Jenkins. Why would Rees Roberts have married a single mother? Once again, for land: Cadrawd asserts that Rees Roberts' farm had in fact come to him through his wife, Peggy's mother, who had inherited it from her father; he in turn had it from his father, whose surname was Mathews and who had taken out the original lease from Edward Mansell (Cadrawd, 1904, p1). Once again there is a hint of a Mansell–Mathew connection. Could Peggy and Iolo have been related through the Mathew family? Cadrawd's version of the story may be supported by the fact that Rees' will required Iolo to pay six pounds per annum to Peggy's widowed mother (Morgan, 2011, p.129).

The obvious response is to wonder whether the source is credible. In fact, he is – and eminently so.

Cadrawd was Thomas Christopher Evans (1846–1918) of Llangynwyd (Roberts, 1953, pp.239–240), the cultural centre of *Tir Iarll*. He had come first in the Aberdare Eisteddfod of 1885 for his collection of Glamorgan folk literature (including many poems in the *Tribannau Morgannwg* metre so beloved by Iolo) and, like his father Thomas (1802–75), was a well-connected folk historian. He was "the principal legatee" of Iolo's material on bardism in Glamorgan and was even known as "a second Iolo" (Löffler, 2007, p.111). Further research in Roberts' papers, which are held at the National Library of Wales, may yield more information about his sources for his account of Iolo's wife, her background, and her land.

12. Llywellyn Traherne and Daniel Jones

There is one more Sheriff of Glamorgan who needs to be discussed: Llywellyn (Llywelyn in other sources) Traherne of Coedrhiglan and St Hilary, who was appointed in 1801. Some sources say that due to a misunderstanding, he was never confirmed in the post, others that he was excused the requirement to take on the office (Williams, 1966, p.29; Moore, 1995, p.93). Either way, he was replaced by Robert Jones of Fonmon (by then the owner of the now-ruinous Boverton Place), whose name appears in the official lists. As we have seen, this might have come as a relief to him. As a forthright Whig, a magistrate, and former Receiver General of Glamorgan, Traherne was a prominent local figure (anon., 1842, p.438). His ancestors had been mid-level government officials, collecting customs fees at Cardiff harbour (Williams, 1966, p.80). One, Edmund (1734–95) had married the heiress of the Coitrahern estate, bringing him substantial properties – and, after her death, he married the heiress of the Coedarhydyglyn estate, bringing even more. Llywellyn Traherne himself had inherited yet more land from his uncle, John Llywellyn, leaving him with about 2,000 acres of land (Jenkins, 1984, p.42).

In 1806 Traherne, aware of the desperate poverty in which Iolo and his family were now living, organised a fund to provide him with a stipend (Jenkins, 2012, pp.235–6). The contributors to the fund were a group of around thirty local gentlemen, each of whom contributed either a guinea or half a guinea annually for the next eighteen years. As we have seen, a guinea was worth 21 shillings, and Iolo himself had said that three and a half shillings per day would provide a comfortable lifestyle. One guinea would thus last for about a week, and it would provide a more economical lifestyle for longer. Traherne's fund was by no means a huge sum, but it would have been important to Iolo.

Once again, though, it is peculiar that nobody seems to have asked the obvious question: why did Llywellyn Traherne do this?

Suggett (2009, p.216) provides a hint. He notes that Iolo had in 1789 attributed the magnificent carved porch at Beaupre Castle, not far from Cowbridge, to Inigo Jones, but by 1797, he was telling a new story. Now he claimed that it was the work of "William Twrch", a local mason with an exotic backstory of travel, romance, and Glamorgan talent (Nicholas, 1874, pp.70–71; Suggett, 2009, p.222).

Beaupre had been acquired by the Edmondes family in 1755 (Jenkins, 1983, p.56). Llywellyn Traherne had married Charlotte, one of the two daughters of John Edmondes (Nicholas, 1874, pp.185–186). Edmondes had not had a son, so the property had been jointly inherited by the two sisters. When Charlotte died, Llywellyn became joint owner with his sister-in-law, Anna; they sold Beaupre Castle to a successful solicitor, Daniel Jones (Thomas, 2000, p.45).

The sale took place in May 1797. Was it just a coincidence that Iolo had changed his history of Beaupre shortly before this?

The castle at this time was not much of an asset. It was largely in ruins, and even the one remaining habitable part, the home of a tenant farmer, was dilapidated (Thomas, 2000, p.43).

Despite this, it already had grand historical associations: a former owner, Sir Philip Basset, had been the Lord Chief Justice of England at the time of King John. Beaupre was, in local tradition, the place where the Magna Carta was first drawn up, and where the Barons of England met to discuss it (Robertson Spencer, 1913, p.162). King John, it will be recalled, was said to have hidden from the barons at nearby Bonvilston. Traherne does seem to have made an effort to make the most of its value: it was advertised as a "manor" – a term which at that time still had its traditional meaning of being "the administrative centre of an estate" (Encyclopaedia Britannica, 1999) – although whether it actually held that status is questionable at best (Thomas, 2000, p.45). An interesting historical connection and a romantic story can also, of course, add value to a property. If Iolo's revised backstory for the porch had helped Llewellyn Traherne get a better price for the sale, then Traherne would certainly have had a motive to repay the favour a few years later. The relationship was a lasting one, too: Llywellyn's son, the Reverend John Montgomery Traherne (Roberts, 1908, p.532), was also a supporter of both Iolo and his son Taliesin (Williams, 1956, p.11).

There is another aspect to the story which adds further insight. Daniel Jones, the purchaser of Beaupre Castle, was originally from Llantwit Major. His wife Louisa, whom he had married the year before he bought Beaupre, was one of the daughters of Whitlock Nicholl of the Ham – and was thus the sister of the Reverend John Nicholl of Remenham and sister-in-law of the Honourable Mary Nicholl (Burke, 1900, p.1172) – who were, at that point, on the verge of moving to Cowbridge themselves. Although the Nicholls were, by this time, one of the leading families of the Glamorgan gentry, Jones himself was of humbler stock. By associating himself with a grand history at Beaupre, he would be establishing himself in continuity with the ancient Marcher past – and, as we will see, the up-and-coming new gentry of the late eighteenth century were very keen to do this. Given his reputation as an antiquarian, Iolo's revised history of the porch at Beaupre would therefore have suited both parties to the sale very nicely indeed.

13. A Mother's Aspirations

As we discussed previously, Edward Williams and Ann Matthews married in 1744. Ann had been living as one of the gentry, with an education paid for by her cousin Elizabeth. She met her husband while she was giving medical assistance to the local population, an act of charity for which she had been trained by her aunt Wenllian. Ann must have worried about whether she would ever find a husband and raise a family, and it would have been a huge relief to finally settle down in a home of her own; the price, of course, was a substantial drop in both economic and social status. Having her first child would have brought great joy – a joy mirrored by the sorrow when her daughter died before her first birthday.

Then came Iolo. In her son, Ann would have seen a way of restoring the family's status amongst the gentry. Although she and Edward would go on to have three more sons, by the social rules of the time those sons would have to make their own way in the world. Iolo, though, as the eldest son, had the potential to restore Ann in her old age to the kind of life she had enjoyed in her youth – if only he could be properly prepared. The three younger brothers could therefore go to the public school to enjoy the basic education that it provided to the children of working families, but if he were to learn the ways and manners of the gentry, she would need to educate Iolo herself.

Iolo's picture of his childhood in *Poems, Lyrical and Pastoral* – of being kept away from school because of his fragile health, and of never being separated from his doting, saintly mother – may contain elements of truth. However, as we have seen, Mary Robinson wrote about her own childhood in extremely similar terms, and so it must be suspected that Iolo was writing to obey a literary convention more than to provide an accurate account. Equally, the picture that has been painted of Ann Matthews as being a clingy, overprotective mother is likely to be inaccurate and unfair. Her husband, Edward Williams, may have been a good man and a talented stonecutter, but he would never be able to improve the family's social status. Iolo was her favourite child because Iolo could provide her way back to polite society.

Unfortunately for her, her plan did not work. She died relatively young at the age of 57; Iolo was still only 23, too young to have achieved the success she would have wanted. Even if she had lived longer, her plans would probably have failed because treating Iolo so plainly as her favourite and educating him as a gentleman whilst he grew up in a craftsman's environment had endowed Iolo with psychological flaws that would plague him for the rest of his life, and which would undermine all of his efforts to restore his family to the level of even minor gentry.

Psychiatrist Ellen Webber Libby (2010) describes how being a mother's favourite child can lead to four major negative consequences in later life.

Firstly, they can be driven to live their life according to their mother's aspirations, rather than making decisions that might be better suited to their own personality and circumstances. Secondly, she says, they tend to lack the basic skills for being an independent adult, having grown up paying more attention to doing what their parent wants rather than looking after their own needs. Children who are less favoured usually turn out to be more practical. Thirdly, having grown up as the favourite, a child is psychologically prepared to assume that the world will look after them in the way that the parent did, and that life will naturally turn out as they wish. Finally, favourite children tend to be indulged and forgiven for bad behaviour to a greater extent than their siblings. This can lead to a lack of responsibility and of an understanding of social boundaries.

All of these behavioural patterns can be observed in Iolo's life. In 1773, for example, while on a visit to north Wales, he collected subscriptions for a collection of Glamorgan poetry, but he never produced it; perhaps he was thinking that he could just get away with it because he had never been properly held to account as a child. Throughout his life, he overstepped social boundaries; on a number of occasions, for example, he got into trouble for writing scurrilous verses about people he disliked.

His three brothers went on to become successful in their craft, with one – Thomas – establishing a successful workshop in Somerset before migrating to Jamaica to join the other two, John and Miles, who had gone there some years previously. All three of these brothers prospered.

Iolo, however, could never settle. It would have been possible for him to rise again to the gentry; indeed, one could say that he *should* have done so. Although biographies of Iolo focus on his poverty – in part, of course, due to the persona he himself adopted in his self-promotion campaign – he clearly was able to raise significant funds at various points in his career. He did, after all, buy a ship (although it sank). He was able to open a quarry on the Margam estate and hire workers; he was able to open a workshop, and later a shop. As we have seen, his marriage to Peggy Roberts brought him land which was already bringing in a not-inconsiderable rental income. Unlike his brothers, he just seems to have not been capable of managing money, turning what should have been a modest but comfortable income into debts that he could not pay.

Suitor et al. (2017) found that being a mother's favourite child is strongly connected to depression in adult life, and this may be linked to Libby's conclusion that a favourite child will pursue their parent's dreams rather than their own. There are certain patterns in Iolo's life that reflect his grandparents. His maternal grandfather was a tax collector; Iolo would apply for a post as a customs officer. His grandfather was ruined by aristocratic abuse of power; Iolo would be a lifelong advocate of justice, and of the rights of the gentry over those of aristocrats. His mother's friends, who were his own childhood tutors, were men of learning and poetry, so Iolo, too, became a man of learning. Iolo seems to have spent his life trying to equal the achievements of his mother's family – and, in the process, spread himself too thin, never quite managing to establish himself. Of course, as we have seen with the Prince of Wales, his pride and inflexibility also undermined him even when he might have succeeded. This constant sense of never living up to his mother's dreams may well have contributed to the fits of depression that he experienced and which, while in London, led him to consider suicide.

It is hard not to conclude that Ann Matthews' efforts to prepare her son to be a gentleman were, ultimately, counterproductive. Her tutoring him in his "rightful" status made him oversensitive to any perceived slight, while the high aims she set for him, based on her own family background, prevented him from discovering his way in life in a more organic manner.

14. Iolo Morganwg as a Member of the Gentry

We can now tie these disparate stories into a coherent picture.

Iolo Morganwg needs to be placed in the context of the gentry of Glamorgan, and in particular with the network of families associated with Cowbridge and the surrounding Vale.

Through his mother's paternal line, Iolo belonged to a family which had been powerful and influential in Glamorgan for many generations. They remained so during his lifetime and were known to look out for relatives who had come down in the world. His maternal grandfather was a landowner who lost everything in a factional conflict with the mighty Mansells of Margam, who were closely connected with the Crown. His maternal grandmother may well have been one of the Williams family of Aberpergwm, through whom Iolo got to know Dafydd Nicolas.

Edward Mathew's misfortune led to his daughter going to live with the Seys family, which links Iolo to "Perdita": Mary Robinson. It meant that Ann Matthews became the neighbour, and friend, of Whitlock Nicholl, whose brother introduced Iolo to John Bradford, and whose son and daughter-in-law introduced him to aristocrats and, possibly, to royalty. She was also a neighbour of the Edwin family, who had royal connections of their own. Ann Mathew's family networks also meant that she would have known the Edwins of Llanmihangel, whose heir Thomas Wyndham more probably provided Iolo's introduction to the Prince of Wales.

While Ann Matthews had no better option than to marry a mason, she would have wanted to give Iolo the best possible chance to rise back up to his grandfather's status. Iolo's ancestry through his mother meant that he grew up knowing the local gentry and, in the Welsh manner, being accepted as one of them.

After years of living on the kindness of others, wondering whether she would ever find a husband or have a family of her own, and after tragically losing her first child at the age of 31 or 32 (Jenkins, 2012, p.5), Iolo would naturally have been precious to Ann, and this partly explains why he was always her favourite – but not entirely. By the standards of the time Iolo, as the eldest son, was the most important: in the families of the gentry, younger sons did not inherit and had to make their own way in the world. Ann would have viewed her own children in the same way, and she did everything she could to prepare Iolo to restore the family's fortunes. This was not pretentiousness or self-conceit (ibid., p.12); she was trying to make a gentleman of him. This is how so many local gentlemen came to be involved in his education: his godfather and namesake, Edward Williams of

Llancarfan; Thomas Richard, the curate of Coychurch (the parish in which Edward Mathew had lived); and John Walters, Rector of Llandough. These men were all important in the society of their day; they did not give their time and their knowledge to just any child – and yet they did for Iolo because he was one of their own class and because his mother was their friend.

On these terms, he courted the heiress of the Deere family but was turned down because he had no property. He was able to marry another heiress, perhaps because her illegitimacy discouraged other suitors. After his marriage, he worked hard at the kind of business ventures which not uncommonly led to status as a gentleman but, unfortunately for him and his family, without success. This may very well have been the result of the psychological consequences of being his mother's favourite.

Before his marriage, he was able to be a carefree mason-poet, mixing with relatively well-off, educated men such as Dafydd Nicholas, tutor and house poet to the Williams family; the land-steward and businessman John Bradford; and Lewis Hopkin, who had a farm (and a farmhouse full of books) as well as a shop (Williams, 1965, pp.30–31). These were all men who had, from humble beginnings, achieved success in life. Following his marriage, Iolo sought to emulate their career paths as builder, entrepreneur, and scholar – but he failed to match their success. If he had managed to succeed, his ancestry, and his wife's land, would have raised him back to gentry status.

Iolo was related to Members of Parliament for Glamorgan and was an active campaigner for others. In the parliamentary election of 1789, he joined with the Mathews, Williams, and Deere families, and other Whigs, in promoting a local gentleman and member of the Edwin family, Wyndham of Dunraven, against the candidate of the aristocratic, royalist Tories. When he began his quest to publish his poetry, the Glamorgan gentry were among his early supporters and subscribers, and they introduced him to other people in Bristol and Bath.

During his second stay in London, Iolo mixed with, and joined in sophisticated debate with, a highly educated network, many of whom were themselves drawn from the aristocracy and gentry. Here there would have been none of the simple artisan who sought subscriptions; here, he would have used the manners and discourse of the gentleman he was raised to be.

Afterwards, his aspirations crushed by the Prince of Wales – perhaps because of the machinations of Mary Nicholl, who played upon Iolo's connection with "Perdita" to turn the prince against him, but more certainly because of his own pig-headedness – Iolo returned to Glamorgan, becoming increasingly focused on promoting his gorsedd and on involvement with Unitarianism, whilst working once more as a stonemason, a profession that became more burdensome with his advancing age. As he slipped further into poverty, his friends amongst the local gentry rallied to his support, with Llywellyn Traherne leading the way – perhaps because Iolo had helped him obtain a higher price for the sale of Beaupre Castle. As with the Edwins and Wyndhams of Llanmihangel and the Nicholls of the Ham, this support spanned generations, with Llywellyn's son helping to support both Iolo and Iolo's son.

Since thirty people contributed generously to Traherne's fund, Iolo must still have been well-regarded amongst the Glamorgan gentry. This makes no sense in the accepted narrative of Iolo as a "plebian radical" (Jenkins, 1983, p.187). It does, however, make sense when we consider him as a fallen member of the gentry; a man whose family had been closely aligned for generations with other local families in political struggle against over-mighty aristocrats and Tories, and whose downfall was a direct result of that shared struggle. A radical he may have become, but he was gentry-born, and the gentry friends of his grandfather and mother looked out for him to the end of his life. Indeed, he socialised with them throughout his life (Malkin, 1807, p.199; Morgan, 1975, p.19). Radical though he was, his views on many topics would not have differed from many of his class. He was no democrat, for example: he did not believe in universal suffrage for men (Jenkins, 2012, p.98), and his support for women's participation in public affairs was limited at best (Charnell-White, 2009, p.361).

His final contribution to the society in which he had been formed came just a few years before his death, when he once again lent his bardic talents to support the local gentry against an aristocrat-backed candidate in the Glamorgan election of 1818 (Jenkins, 2012, p.232), echoing his efforts of almost three decades earlier.

Looking at Iolo's life in this way, it fits into a pattern, which began with his grandfather, in a struggle for the rights of the local gentry – those who truly belonged to his beloved Glamorgan – against the power of the throne, the central government, and the aristocracy. It was these who threw down his family from that status to working with their hands, and it was they, in the form of the Prince of Wales, combined with the character flaws so counterproductively established by his mother, who ultimately prevented him from restoring his family's former fortunes and status.

Through his Seys connection, Iolo belonged to an ancient line that died out during the social changes of the eighteenth century. Through his Mathew and Williams ancestry, he was connected to old families that managed to successfully navigate that social transition. Through his efforts on behalf of the Wyndham campaign, he was connected to "new" gentry who needed "ancient" family histories to legitimise themselves locally, and as a highly respected antiquarian and scholar, he was just the man to help them do that.

Scholars have often wondered why Iolo became so deeply involved in forging histories and literature. While Jenkins (2009, p.18) justifies him as "a child of his age", part of a wider trend of national myth-building across Europe, nobody has pointed out that, much closer to home, Iolo was mixing with new entrants to Glamorgan society who were very keen indeed to acquire newly-minted pedigrees connecting them to ancient families, and who then insinuated these new pedigrees into the emerging society directories such as Burke (Jones, 1976, p.28). A well-respected but impecunious antiquarian scholar might, perhaps, have profited from this need. Although there is no evidence to show that Iolo was involved in this, he would have been the perfect candidate. This, perhaps, explains much about why he created forgeries more generally: he was doing for his beloved nation what the incoming gentry were doing for themselves – and he could see that it was effective. This also places him firmly in the social networks of gentry society, many of whom would have seen him as belonging there as much as, or even more than, they did.

References

Altschul, M. (1971). 'Glamorgan and Morgannwg Under the Rule of the De Clare Family'. In Pugh, T.B. (ed.), *Glamorgan County History Vol. III: The Middle Ages*. Cardiff: Glamorgan County History Committee, pp.45–72.

ancientmonuments.uk. (n.d.). *Medieval Chapel of Talygarn, Pont-y-clun, Rhondda, Cynon, Taff (Rhondda Cynon Taf)*. [online] Available at: https://ancientmonuments.uk/130464-medieval-chapel-of-talygarn-pont-y-clun [Accessed 16 Jan. 2022].

Anon. (1830). 'Family Notices'. *The Monmouthshire Merlin*. [online] 7 Aug., p.3. Available at: <https://newspapers.library.wales/view/3390916/3390919/21/> [Accessed 22 Oct. 2021].

Anon. (1842). Llewellyn Traherne, Esq. in Urban, S. (ed.) *The Gentleman's Magazine* XVII (April). London: William Pickering, John Bowyer Nichols and Son. [online] Available at: <https://www.google.co.uk/

books/edition/The_Gentleman_s_Magazine/Lab-PAAAAMAAJ?hl=en&gbpv=1&pg=PA438&printsec-=frontcover> [Accessed 26 Oct. 2021].

Anon. (1863a). 'Glamorgan Pedigrees: Seys of Boverton'. *The Cardiff and Merthyr Guardian.* [online] 10 Jul., p.8. Available at: <https://newspapers.library.wales/view/3093641/3093649/57> [Accessed 21 Oct. 2021].

Anon. (1863b). 'Glamorgan Pedigrees: Seys of Boverton'. *The Cardiff and Merthyr Guardian.* [online] 17 Jul., p.8. Available at: <https://newspapers.library.wales/view/3093650/3093658> [Accessed 21 Oct. 2021].

Anon. (n.d.a). 'Location: Parish (Church): Llangyfelach'. *The Clergy of the Church of England Database.* [online] Available at: <https://theclergydatabase.org.uk/jsp/locations/index.jsp?locUnitKey=27607> [Accessed 27 Oct. 2021].

Anon. (n.d.b). 'Person: Carne, Charles (1729 – 1764)'. *The Clergy of the Church of England Database.* [online] Available at: <https://theclergydatabase.org.uk/jsp/persons/CreatePersonFrames.jsp?PersonID=11589> [Accessed 21 Oct. 2021].

Anon. (n.d.c). 'Person: Jones, John (1795 – 1827)'. *The Clergy of the Church of England Database.* [online] Available at: <https://theclergydatabase.org.uk/jsp/persons/CreatePersonFrames.jsp?PersonID=131782> [Accessed 08 May 2022].

Anon (n.d.d.). Person: Nicholl, Illtyd (1767 – 1788). *The Clergy of the Church of England Database.* [online] Available at: <https://theclergydatabase.org.uk/jsp/persons/CreatePersonFrames.jsp?PersonID=37202> [Accessed 31 Dec. 2021].

Anon. (1991). 'The Mathew Family'. In Anon., *"Twixt Chain and Gorge": A History of Radyr and Morganstown.* Radyr: Radyr and Morganstown New Horizons History Group. pp.20–36.

Anon. (2008a). 'GENTRY and LANDLORDS'. In J. Davies, N. Jenkins, M. Baines, et al., *The Welsh Academy Encyclopaedia of Wales.* Cardiff: Literature Wales. [online] Available from: <https://search.credoreference.com/content/entry/waencywales/gentry_and_landlords/0?institutionId=1794> [Accessed 25 Oct. 2021].

Ahmed, R. (2022). *The hidden spot in Cardiff that marks the start of a medieval pilgrimage.* WalesOnline. [online] Available at: <https://www.walesonline.co.uk/news/wales-news/penrhys-pilgrimage-way-walking-cardiff-22830606> [Accessed 9 Feb. 2022].

Anon. (2008b). 'LLANDOW (Llandŵ), Vale of Glamorgan (1594 ha; 754 inhabitants)'. In J. Davies, N. Jenkins, M. Baines et al., *The Welsh Academy Encyclopaedia of Wales.* Cardiff: Literature Wales. [online] Available from: <https://search.credoreference.com/content/entry/waencywales/llandow_lland%C5%B5_vale_of_glamorgan_1594_ha_754_inhabitants/0?institutionId=1794> [Accessed 22 Oct. 2021].

Anon. (2008c). 'TALBOT Family Landowners'. In J. Davies, N. Jenkins, M. Baines & et. al., *The Welsh Academy Encyclopaedia of Wales*. Cardiff: Literature Wales. [online] Available from: <https://search.credoreference.com/content/entry/waencywales/talbot_family_landowners/0?institutionId=1794> [Accessed 25 Oct. 2021].

Anon. (2016). *Traherne Dynasty*. www.llantrisant.net. [online] Available at: <https://www.llantrisant.net/index.php/freemen/notable-freemen/125-freeman/notable-freemen/463-traherne-dynasty> [Accessed 26 Oct. 2021].

Anon. (2020). Jesus College Archives: Papers of Joseph Hoare (PR. 1768–1802). [online] Available at: <https://www.jesus.ox.ac.uk/wp-content/uploads/2021/04/Archives-JCPR18.pdf> (Accessed 16 Jan. 2022).

Baker, M. & Eadsforth, C. (2011). 'Agency reversal and the steward's lot when discharge exceeds charge: English archival evidence, 1739–1890'. *Accounting History* 16(1): 87–109.

Beckett, J.V. (1985). 'Land Tax or Excise: The Levying of Taxation in Seventeenth- and Eighteenth-Century England'. *The English Historical Review* 100(395): 285–308.

Beckett, J.V. & Turner, M. (1990). Taxation and Economic Growth in Eighteenth-Century England. *The Economic History Review* 45(3): 377–403.

Berkeleyparks. (n.d.). Ham Manor Park - Residential Park in Llantwit Major. [online] Available at: <https://berkeleyparks.co.uk/park-category/ham-manor/> [Accessed 22 Oct. 2021].

Bradley, A.G. (1909). *Highways and Byways in North Wales*. London: Macmillan and Co. Limited.

Brown, R.L. (1993). 'Parsons in Perplexity'. *Morgannwg: The Journal of Glamorgan History.* XXXVII: 56–82.

Bryant, D. (1912). 'The Marcher Lordship of Glamorgan'. In Bryant, D., Phillips, J.L. and Prosser, H., *Historical Sketches of Glamorgan*, vol. II. London and Cardiff: Western Mail, Limited.

Bullion, J.L. (2004). Augusta [Princess Augusta of Saxe-Gotha], Princess of Wales (1719–1772), Consort of Frederick Lewis, Prince of Wales. *Oxford Dictionary of National Biography.* [online] Available at: <https://www.oxforddnb.com/view/10.1093/ref:odnb/9780198614128.001.0001/odnb-9780198614128-e-46829> [Accessed 24 Dec. 2021].

Burke, B. (1900). *A Genealogical and Heraldic History of the Landed Gentry of Great Britain*. 10th ed. London: Harrison & Sons.

Burke, B. & Burke, A.P. (1915). *A Genealogical and Heraldic History of the Peerage and Baronetage, the Privy Council, Knightage and Privy Council*. 77th ed. London: Harrison & Sons.

Burke, J. & Burke, J.B. (1838). *A Genealogical and Heraldic History of the Extinct and Dormant Baronetcies of England*. London: Scott, Webster, and Geary.

Byrne, P. (2004). *Perdita: The Life of Mary Robinson*. London: Harper Perennial.

Cadrawd (1904). 'Welsh Tit-Bits Neu Wreichion Oddi-ar Yr Eigion'. *The Cardiff Times*, 17 Dec., p.1. [online] Available at: <https://newspapers.library.wales/view/3427556> [Accessed 22 Oct. 2021].

Cave, E. ed., (1813). *The Gentleman's Magazine: Or, Monthly Intelligencer. Volume the first [-fifth], for the year 1731 [-1735]*. [online] Available at: <https://www.google.co.uk/books/edition/The_Gentleman_s_Magazine_Or_Monthly_Inte/Yq8UAAAAQAA-J?hl=en&gbpv=1&dq=first+viscount+ashbrook&pg=PA389&printsec=frontcover> [Accessed 22 Oct. 2021].

Charnell-White, C. (2009). 'Women and Gender in the Private and Social Relationships of Iolo Morganwg'. In Jenkins, G.H. (ed). *A Rattleskull Genius: The Many Faces of Iolo Morganwg*. Cardiff: University Of Wales Press, pp. 359–382.

Civil Service Commission (n.d.). *Civil Service History*. [online] Available at: <https://www.civilservicecommission.org.uk/civil-service-history.html> [Accessed 29 Oct. 2021].

Coflein (2021). *Abercynrig*. Royal Commission on the Ancient and Historical Monuments of Wales [online] Available at: <https://coflein.gov.uk/en/site/122/> [Accessed 5 Jan. 2022].

Constantine, M. (2009). 'This Wildernessed Business of Publication: The Making of Poems Lyric and Pastoral (1794)'. In Jenkins, G.H. (ed). *A Rattleskull Genius: The Many Faces of Iolo Morganwg*. Cardiff: University Of Wales Press, pp.123–146.

Cracroft-Brennan, P. (n.d.). *Ashbrook, Viscount (I, 1751)* www.cracroftspeerage.co.uk. [online] Available at: <http://www.cracroftspeerage.co.uk/ashbrook1751.htm> [Accessed 26 May 2022].

Darwall-Smith, R. (2021). *Re: Jesus College and the Rectorship of Remenham*. Email to the author, 6 October.

Davenport, H. (2004). *The Prince's Mistress: a Life of Mary Robinson*. Stroud: Sutton.

Davies, C. (2021). *Re: [NLW English] Prynhawn da,As I am not able to visit the Library's reading rooms at present, I would like to request scanned PDF copies (low resolution) of*. Email to the author, 12 October.

Davies, D.W. (2009). 'At Defiance: Iolo, Godwin, Coleridge, Wordsworth' in Jenkins, G.H. (ed). *A Rattleskull Genius: The Many Faces of Iolo Morganwg*. Cardiff: University Of Wales Press, pp.147–172.

Davies, E.T. (1962). 'From the Restoration to Disestablishment'. In Davies, E.T. (ed.), *The Story of the Church in Glamorgan 560-1960*. London: S.P.C.K., pp.67–87.

Davies, W. Ll. (1959). 'THOMAS, RHYS (1720? – 1790), printer'. *Dictionary of Welsh Biography*. [online] Available at: <https://biography.wales/article/s-THOM-RHY-1720> (Accessed 16 Jan. 2022).

Davies, I. (1967). *"A Certaine Schoole": A History of Cowbridge Grammar School*. Cowbridge: D. Brown and Sons, Ltd.

Day, C. (2013). *Wiltshire Marriage Patterns 1754-1914: Geographical Mobility, Cousin Marriage and Illegitimacy*. Newcastle Upon Tyne: Cambridge Scholars Publisher.

Debrett, J. (1823). *The Peerage of the United Kingdom of Great Britain and Ireland. Vol II: Scotland and Ireland*. 15th ed. London: [s.n.].

Debrett's (n.d.). *Debrett's Guide to the Hierarchy of Titles in the Peerage*. debretts.com. [online] Available at: <https://debretts.com/peerage/ranks-and-privileges-of-the-peerage/> [Accessed 22 Oct. 2021].

dictionary.cambridge.org. (n.d.). 'COUSIN | meaning in the Cambridge English Dictionary' in *Cambridge Dictionary*. [online] Available at: <https://dictionary.cambridge.org/dictionary/english/cousin>

Emanuel, H.D. (1961). 'Llancarfan and St. Cadoc' in Williams, S. (ed.), *The Garden of Wales*. Barry: Stewart Williams, Publishers.

Encyclopædia Britannica (1999). 'Manor house'. *Britannica Academic*. [online] Available at: <https://academic.eb.com/levels/collegiate/article/manor-house/50596> [Accessed 5 Nov. 2021].

Evans, C.J.O. (1943). *Glamorgan: Its History and Topography*. 2nd ed. Cardiff:[s.n.]

Foreman, A. (1998). *Georgiana, Duchess of Devonshire*. London: HarperCollins Publishers.

Gibbs, D.E. (1971). 'Llantwit Major – Medieval and Modern' in Kelly, L.V. (ed), *Llantwit Major: A History and Guide*. Cardiff: The Llantwit Major Local History Society with South Glamorgan County Library. pp.20–28.

Grant, R. (1978). *The Parliamentary History of Glamorgan 1542–1976*. Swansea: Christopher Davies.

Griffith, J. (1904). *Edward II in Glamorgan*. London: W.B. Roberts / Cardiff: Western Mail Limited.

Griffiths, G.M. (1959). 'KEMEYS and KEMEYS-TYNTE family, of Cefn Mabli, Monmouth'. *Dictionary of Welsh Biography*. biography.wales. [online] Available at: <https://biography.wales/article/s-KEME-CEF-1234?&query=baronet&sort=sort_name&page=3> [Accessed 17 Feb. 2022].

Heal, F. & Holmes, C. (1994). *The Gentry in England and Wales 1500–1700*. Basingstoke: MacMillan.

Hill, C.P. (1977). *British Economic and Social History 1700–1975* (4th ed.) London: Edward Arnold.

Hilling, J.B. (1975). 'Cardiff'. In Davey, W.P. (ed.), *South Glamorgan: A County History*. Barry: Stewart Williams, Publishers, pp.38–115.

Hilling, J.B. (1978). *Llandaf Past and Present*. Barry: Stewart Willams, Publishers.

Hopkin-James, L.J. (1922). *Old Cowbridge: Borough, Church, and School*. Cardiff: The Educational Publishing Company, Ltd.

Howell, A. (n.d.). 'What is a High Sheriff?' *Welsh High Sheriff*. [online] Available at: <https://www.highsheriffsouthglamorgan.com/previous-high-sheriff-s> [Accessed 28 Oct. 2021].

Howell, D. W. (1986). *Patriarchs and Parasites: The Gentry of South-West Wales in the Eighteenth Century*. Cardiff: University of Wales Press.

James, B.Ll. (1972). 'The Welsh Language in the Vale of Glamorgan'. *Morgannwg: The Journal of Glamorgan History* XVI: 16–36.

James, B. Ll. (1975). 'Llantwit Major'. In Davey, W.P. (ed.), *South Glamorgan: A County History*. Barry: Stewart Williams, Publishers, pp.205–224.

James, B. Ll. & Frances, D.J. (1979). *Cowbridge and Llanblethian: Past and Present.* Barry: Stewart Williams, Publishers.

Jarvis, B. (2009). 'Iolo Morganwg and the Welsh Cultural Background'. In Jenkins, G.H. (ed). *A Rattleskull Genius: The Many Faces of Iolo Morganwg.* Cardiff: University Of Wales Press, pp.29–49.

Jenkins, G.H. (2009). 'The Unitarian Firebrand, the Cambrian Society and the Eisteddfod'. In Jenkins, G.H. (ed). *A Rattleskull Genius: The Many Faces of Iolo Morganwg.* Cardiff: University Of Wales Press, pp.269–292.

Jenkins, G.H. (2012). *Bard of Liberty: The Political Radicalism of Iolo Morganwg.* Cardiff: University Of Wales Press.

Jenkins, G.H. (2018). *Y Digymar Iolo Morganwg.* Talybont: Y Lolfa.

Jenkins, J.P. (1979). 'From Edward Lhuyd to Iolo Morganwg: The Death and Rebirth of Glamorgan Antiquarianism'. *Morgannwg: The Journal of Glamorgan History* XXIII: 29–47.

Jenkins, P. (1983). *The Making of a Ruling Class: The Glamorgan gentry 1640 – 1790.* Cambridge: Cambridge University Press.

Jenkins, P. (1984). 'The Creation of an "Ancient Gentry": Glamorgan 1760-1840'. *Welsh History Review Cylchgrawn Hanes Cymru.* 12(1): 29–49.

Jenkins, R.T. (1954). 'WILLIAMS (TEULU), Aberpergwm, Glyn Nedd'. In Lloyd, J.E., Jenkins, R.T. and Davies, W.Ll. (eds.). *Y Bywgraffiadur Cymreig Hyd 1940*. Llundain: Anrhydeddus Gymdeithas y Cymmrodorion.

Jenkins, R. T. (1959a). 'EDWIN family, of Llanfihangel or 'Llanmihangel', Glamorganshire'. *Dictionary of Welsh Biography*. [online] Available at: <https://biography.wales/article/s-EDWI-LLA-1642> [Accessed 24 Dec. 2021].

Jenkins, R.T. (1959b). 'WILLIAMS family, of Aberpergwm, Vale of Neath.' *Dictionary of Welsh Biography*. biography. wales. [online] Available at: <https://biography.wales/article/s-WILL-ABE-1500> [Accessed 22 Oct. 2021].

John, R. (1966). 'The Sheriffs of Glamorgan'. In Williams, G., *A List of the Names and Residences of the High Sheriffs of the County of Glamorgan from 1541 to 1966*. [s.l.]: [s.n.] pp.11–16.

Jones, A. (1955). *The Story of Glamorgan*. Llandybie: Llyfrau'r Dryw.

Jones, C.W. (2009). 'Iolo Morganwg and the Welsh Rural Landscape'. In Jenkins, G.H. (ed). *A Rattleskull Genius: The Many Faces of Iolo Morganwg*. Cardiff: University Of Wales Press, pp.227–250.

Jones, F. (1976). 'The Old Families of Wales'. In Moore, D. (ed.), *Wales in the Eighteenth Century*. Swansea: Christopher Davies (Publishers) Ltd. pp.27–46.

Jones, Ff.M. (2010). *"The Bard is a Very Singular Character": Iolo Morganwg Marginalia and Print culture.* Cardiff: University Of Wales Press.

Jones, G.E. (1984). *Modern Wales: A Concise History c.1485–1979.* Cambridge: Cambridge University Press.

Kelly, L.V. (1971). 'The Ham and Ty Mawr'. In Kelly, L.V. (ed.), *Llantwit Major: A History and Guide.* Cardiff: The Llantwit Major Local History Society with South Glamorgan County Library. pp.47–50.

Lemmings, D. (2004). 'King, Peter, first Baron King (1669–1734), lord chancellor.' *Oxford Dictionary of National Biography.* [online] Available at: <https://www.oxforddnb.com/view/10.1093/ref:odnb/9780198614128.001.0001/odnb-9780198614128-e-15582> [Accessed 22 Oct. 2021].

Levi, P. (n.d.). 'Beaumont 1861 – 1961'. [online] Available at: < https://www.beaumont-union.co.uk/school.html> [Accessed 27 May 2022]

Lewis, C.W. (1971). 'The Literary Tradition of Morgannwg Down to the Middle of the Sixteenth Century'. In Williams, S. (ed.), *Glamorgan Historian Volume Two.* Barry: Stewart Williams, pp.449–554.

Lewis, C.W. (2004a). 'Bradford, John [Siôn] (1706–1785), poet and antiquary.' *Oxford Dictionary of National Biography.* [online] Available at: <https://www.oxforddnb.com/view/10.1093/ref:odnb/9780198614128.001.0001/odnb-9780198614128-e-3176> [Accessed 16 Jan. 2022].

Lewis, C.W. (2004b). 'Nicolas, Dafydd (bap. 1705?, d. 1774), poet and schoolmaster.' [online] Available at: <https://www.oxforddnb.com/view/10.1093/ref:odnb/9780198614128.001.0001/odnb-9780198614128-e-20096> [Accessed 22 Oct. 2021].

Libby, E.W. (2010). '4 Reasons Why Being Your Parent's Favorite Can Hold You Back'. *Psychology Today*. [online] Available at: <https://www.psychologytoday.com/us/blog/the-favorite-child/201002/4-reasons-why-being-your-parents-favorite-can-hold-you-back> [Accessed 6 Dec. 2021].

Löffler, M. (2007). *The Literary and Historical Legacy of Iolo Morganwg 1826–1926*. Cardiff: University Of Wales Press.

Mackworth, H. (1707). *The case of Sir Humphrey Mackworth, and the mine adventurers with respect to the extraordinary proceedings of the agents, servants and dependents, of the Right Honourable Sir Thomas Mansell, Bar*. London. NLW 99370214102419. [online] Available at: <http://hdl.handle.net/10107/5285355>.

Malkin, B.H. (1807). *The Scenery, Antiquities, and Biography, of South Wales* (Vol I). London: Longman, Hurst, Rees and Orne.

Martin, J. (1979). 'Estate Stewards and their Work in Glamorgan, 1660–1760'. *Morgannwg: The Journal of Glamorgan History* XXIII: 9–28.

Maynard Bridge, F. (1922). *Princes of Wales*. London: H. F. W. Deane and Sons.

Mee, J. (2009). "Images of New Truth Born': Iolo, William Blake, and the Literary Radicalism of the 1790s'. In Jenkins, G.H. (ed.). *A Rattleskull Genius: The Many Faces of Iolo Morganwg*. Cardiff: University Of Wales Press, pp.173–198.

Merrick, R. (1983). *Morganiae Archaiographia: A Book of the Antiquities of Glamorganshire*. James, B. Ll. (ed.) South Glamorgan: South Wales Record Society.

Mitford, J. (ed.) (1847). 'VISCOUNT ASHBROOK'. *The Gentleman's Magazine: and historical review, July 1856-May 1868*. London. [online] Available at: <http://ezproxy.lib.le.ac.uk/login?url=https://www.proquest.com/historical-periodicals/viscount-ashbrook/docview/8494839/se-2> [Accessed 27 May 2022].

Moore, P. (1975). 'Penarth'. In Davey, W.P. (ed.), *South Glamorgan: A County History*. Barry: Stewart Williams, Publishers, pp.116–138.

Moore, P. (ed.) (1995). *Glamorgan Sheriffs: Biographical Notes on Sheriffs 1966-1993 and Lists of Sheriffs from the Twelfth Century to the Present Day*. Cardiff: University Of Wales Press on behalf of the Glamorgan County History Trust.

Morgan, P. (2011). "A Kind of Sacred Land': Iolo Morganwg and Monmouthshire'. In Burton, A.M. and Williams, D.H. (eds.) *The Monmouthshire Antiquary: Proceedings of the Monmouthshire Antiquarian Association* XXVII: 127–134.

Morrill, J. (2004). 'Cromwell, Oliver (1599–1658), Lord Protector of England, Scotland, and Ireland.' *Oxford Dictionary of National Biography.* [online] Available at: <https://www.oxforddnb.com/view/10.1093/ref:odnb/9780198614128.001.0001/odnb-9780198614128-e-6765> [Accessed 9 Jan. 2022].

Morris, A. (1907). *Glamorgan.* Newport: John E. Southall.

Morgan, P. (1975). *Iolo Morganwg.* Cardiff: University of Wales Press on behalf of the Welsh Arts Council.

Murphy, G.M. (2004) 'Malkin, Benjamin Heath (1770–1842), schoolmaster and antiquary.' *Oxford Dictionary of National Biography.* [online] Available at: <https://www.oxforddnb.com/view/10.1093/ref:odnb/9780198614128.001.0001/odnb-9780198614128-e-17885> [Accessed 5 Dec. 2021].

Nicholas, T. (1872). *Annals and Antiquities of the Counties and County Families of Wales.* London: Longmans. Reprint, Barry: Stewart Williams (n.d.) [online] Available at: <https://www.google.co.uk/books/edition/Annals_and_Antiquities_of_the_Counties_a/Y1IBAAAAQAAJ?hl=en> [Accessed 28 Oct. 2021].

Nicholas, T. (1874). *The History and Antiquities of Glamorganshire and its Families.* London: Longmans, Green & Co.

Oak, W. (1974). 'Old Neath in Pictures'. In Jenkins, E. (ed.), *Neath and District: A Symposium.* Neath: Elis Jenkins, pp.67–72.

Ogwen Williams, W. (1960). 'The Union of England and Wales'. In Roderick, A.J. (ed.), *Wales Through the Ages Volume II: Modern Wales*. Llandybie: Christopher Davies (Publishers) Ltd. pp.16–23.

Orr, M. (2001). 'Dettingen, battle of'. In *The Oxford Companion to Military History*. Oxford: Oxford University Press. [online] Available at: <https://www.oxfordreference.com/view/10.1093/acref/9780198606963.001.0001/acref-9780198606963-e-371> [Accessed 26 May 2022].

Outhwaite, R.B. (1973). 'Age at Marriage in England from the Late Seventeenth to the Nineteenth Century'. *Transactions of the Royal Historical Society* 23: 55–70.

Parkinson, E. (ed.) (1994). *The Glamorganshire Hearth Tax Assessment of 1670*. Cardiff: South Wales Record Society.

Picard, L. (2000). *Dr. Johnson's London*. London: Wiedenfeld & Nicolson.

Pugh, T.B. (1971). 'The Ending of the Middle Ages'. In Pugh, T.B. (ed.), *Glamorgan County History Vol. III: The Middle Ages*. Cardiff: Glamorgan County History Committee, pp.555–581.

Remenham Parish (n.d.). *The Church of St Nicholas, Remenham*. [online] Available at: <https://www.remenhamparish.org.uk/remenham-church/history/> [Accessed 22 Oct. 2021].

Royal Collection Trust (n.d.). *Mary Hamilton and the Prince of Wales*. www.rct.uk. [online] Available at: <https://www.rct.uk/collection/georgian-papers-programme/mary-hamilton-and-the-prince-of-wales> [Accessed 8 May 2022].

Rhys, J. & Brynmore-Jones, D. (1923). *The Welsh People*. London: T. Fisher Unwin Ltd.

Richards, J.W. (1994). *The Xenophobe's Guide to the Welsh*. Horsham: Ravette Publishing.

Roberts, E.P. (1953). 'Evans, Thomas Christopher'. In Lloyd, J.E., Jenkins, R.T. and Davies, W.Ll. (eds.). *Y Bywgraffiadur Cymreig Hyd 1940*. Llundain: Anrhydeddus Gymdeithas y Cymmrodorion.

Roberts, M.J.D., Finn, M., & Wrightson, K. (2004). *Making English Morals: Voluntary Association and Moral Reform in England, 1787–1886*. Cambridge: Cambridge University Press.

Robinson, W.R.B. (1987). 'Knighted Welsh Landowners, 1458–1558: A Provisional List' in *The Welsh History Review Cylchgrawn Hanes Cymru* 13(3):282–298.

Roberts, T.R. (1908). *Eminent Welshmen*. Cardiff & Merthyr Tydfil: The Educational Publishing Company, Ltd.

Robertson Spencer, M. (1913). *Annals of South Glamorgan*. Carmarthen: W. Spurrel and Son. Reprint, Barry: Stewart Williams, 1970.

Sanders, R. (n.d.). 'A Brief History of Methodism in Glamorgan'. *Cardiff & Glamorgan Family History Research*. [online] Available at: <http://www.glamorganfamilyhistory.co.uk/METHOD.html> [Accessed 8 May 2022].

Scott Archer, M. (1970). *The Welsh Post Towns Before 1840*. Chichester: Phillimore & Co. Ltd.

Shrievalty Association, The (n.d.). *History of High Sheriffs*. High Sheriffs' Association. [online] Available at: <https://highsheriffs.com/about/history-of-high-sheriffs/> [Accessed 25 Oct. 2021].

Smith, J.B. (1971). 'The Kingdom of Morgannwg and the Norman Conquest of Glamorgan'. In Pugh, T.B. (ed.), *Glamorgan County History Vol. III: The Middle Ages*. Cardiff: Glamorgan County History Committee, pp.1–44.

sthilary.org.uk. (n.d.). *New Beaupre*. [online] Available at: <https://sthilary.org.uk/history/newbeaupre> [Accessed 26 Oct. 2021].

Suggett, R. (2009). 'Iolo Morganwg: Stonecutter, Builder and Antiquary'. In Jenkins, G.H. (ed). *A Rattleskull Genius: The Many Faces of Iolo Morganwg*. Cardiff: University Of Wales Press, pp.197–226.

Suitor, J.J., Gilligan, M., Peng, S.Y., Jung, J.H., & Pillemer, K. (2017) 'Role of Perceived Maternal Favoritism and Disfavoritism in Adult Children's Psychological Well-Being'. *The Journals of Gerontology: Series B*. 72 (6): pp.1054–1066.

The Independent. (2008). 'Last day at Tower, the coalmine that became a goldmine'. [online] Available at: <https://www.independent.co.uk/news/uk/this-britain/last-day-at-tower-the-coalmine-that-became-a-goldmine-774530.html> [Accessed 7 Jan. 2022].

Thomas, G. (1974). 'Coal Industry'. In Jenkins, E. (ed.) *Neath and District: A Symposium*. Neath: Elis Jenkins, pp.166–198.

Thomas, H.M. (1997). 'Llanmihangel, near Cowbridge: A Tale of Family Fortunes and Misfortunes'. *Morgannwg: The Journal of Glamorgan History*. XLI: 9–38.

Thomas, H.M. (2000). *St. Hilary: A History of the Place and its People*. St. Hilary: St. Hilary 2000.

Thomas, H.M. (2005). ''With This Ring' - The Importance of the Heiress in the Descent of Three Glamorgan Estates'. *Morgannwg: The Journal of Glamorgan History*. XLIX: 67–78.

Thomas, P.D.G. (n.d.). *Glamorgan | History of Parliament Online*. www.historyofparliamentonline.org. [online] Available at: <https://www.historyofparliamentonline.org/volume/1754-1790/constituencies/glamorgan> [Accessed 9 Jan. 2022].

Thomas, P.D.G. (1960). 'Eighteenth Century Politics'. In Roderick, A.J. (ed.), *Wales Through the Ages Volume II: Modern Wales*. Llandybie: Christopher Davies (Publisher) Ltd., pp.94–100.

Thomas, P.D.G. (1976). 'Society, Government and Politics'. In Moore, D. (ed.), *Wales in the Eighteenth Century*. Swansea: Christopher Davies (Publishers) Ltd., pp.9–26.

Thomas, P.H. (1965). 'Medical Men of Glamorgan'. In Williams, S. (ed.), *Glamorgan Historian Volume Two*. Barry: Stewart Williams, pp.159–173.

Twiston Davies, L. & Edwards, E. (1939). *Welsh Life in the Eighteenth Century*. London: Country Life Ltd.

Vicars, A.E. (ed.) (1908*). Lodge's Peerage, Baronetage, Knightage & Companionage of the British Empire* (77th ed.). London: Kelly's Directories Ltd.

Vickery, A. (2013). 'Mutton Dressed as Lamb? Fashioning Age in Georgian England'. *Journal of British Studies* 52 (October 2013): 858–886.

Waring, E. (1850). *Recollections and Anecdotes of Edward Williams: The Bard of Glamorgan; Or Iolo Morganwg*. London: Charles Gilpin. [online] Available at: <https://www.google.co.uk/books/edition/Recollections_and_Anecdotes_of_Edward_Wi/0OI-IAAAAQAAJ?hl=en&gbpv=1&pg=PA4&printsec=-frontcover> [Accessed 22 Oct. 2021].

Williams, G. (1966). *A List of the Names and Residences of the High Sheriffs of the County of Glamorgan from 1541 to 1966*. [s.l.]: [s.n.]

Williams, G.A. (1965). 'South Wales Radicalism: The First Phase'. In Williams, S. (ed.), *Glamorgan Historian Volume Two*. Barry: Stewart Williams, pp.30–39.

Williams, G.J. (1956). *Iolo Morganwg: Y Gyfrol Gyntaf.* Caerdydd: Gwasg Prifysgol Cymru.

Williams, G. J. (1959a). 'BRADFORD, JOHN (1706 – 1785), weaver, fuller, and dyer'. *Dictionary of Welsh Biography.* [online] Available at: <https://biography.wales/article/s-BRAD-JOH-1706> [Accessed 16 Jan. 2022].

Williams, G.J. (1959b). 'NICOLAS, DAFYDD (1705? – 1774), poet'. *Dictionary of Welsh Biography.* [online] Available at: <https://biography.wales/article/s-NICO-DAF-1705> [Accessed 22 Oct. 2021].

Williams, M.I. (1965). 'Some Aspects of Glamorgan Farming in Pre-Industrial Times'. In Williams, S. (ed.), *Glamorgan Historian Volume Two.* Barry: Stewart Williams, pp.174–185.

Williams, R. (1852). *A Biographical Dictionary of Eminent Welshmen.* Llandovery: William Rees / London: Longman and Co.

Williams, W.Ll. (1919). *The Making of Modern Wales: Studies in the Tudor Settlement of Wales.* London: Macmillan and Co., Limited.

Williams, W.R. (1895). *The Parliamentary History of the Principality of Wales 1541–1895.* Brecknock: Privately Printed for the Author by Edwin Davies and BELL, "County Times" Offices.

Williams ab Ithel, J. (1862). *Barddas; The Bardo-Druidic System of the Isle of Britain*. Llandovery: D.J. Roderick / London: Longman & Co.

www.collinsdictionary.com. (n.d.). 'Cousin-german definition and meaning'. *Collins English Dictionary*. [online] Available at: <https://www.collinsdictionary.com/dictionary/english/cousin-german> [Accessed 22 Oct. 2021].

Index

A

Abercynrig, 27, 67, 93
Aberpergwm, 22, 54–57, 124
Aberysgir, 67
ap Gruffydd Gethin, Ifan, 30
ap Gwaethfoed, 30
    Aidan, 30
    Gwilym, 30
Ash Hall, 104, 107
Ashbrook (Viscounts), 25, 28, 67

B

Barbauld, Anna Laetitia, 86
Beaupre Castle, 116, 117, 118, 127
Blades, Elizabeth. *See* Seys: Elizabeth
Blaenau Morganwg. See Glamorgan
Blake, William, 99, 100
Bosworth (Battle of), 32
Boverton Place, 47, 49, 50, 51, 52, 54, 57, 58, 62, 64, 115
Bradford, John, 45, 71, 125, 126
Brecon, 16, 27, 88, 93
Bristol, 17, 21, 22, 79, 86, 127
Bryn-y-gynnen, 31, 32, 36

C

Cadogan, William, 65
Cadrawd, 56, 111, 112, 113, 114
Cardiff, 22, 31, 33, 49, 54, 56, 58, 68, 81, 96, 112, 113, 115
Carlton House, 9, 10, 75, 103
Carmarthenshire, 16, 23, 33
Carne, Rev. Charles, 59, 68
Caroline of Brunswick, 9, 76
Castell-y-Mynach, 31, 35, 36, 37
Cefn Mably, 81, 88

Charles II, 96
Coal, 15, 16, 22, 40, 56
Coinage reform, 1696, 36
Coleridge, Samuel Taylor, 86
cousin-german, 48, 85
Cowbridge, 7, 22, 42, 51, 61, 62, 65, 66, 72, 73, 95, 96, 97, 98, 99, 100, 101, 102, 116, 118, 124
Cowbridge Grammar School, 7, 61, 72, 95
Coychurch, 30, 33, 35, 36, 37, 126
Cromwell, Oliver, 25, 55
Cwrt Bleddyn, 89

D
Darby, Mary. *See* Robinson: Mary
Darwall-Smith, Dr. Robin, 7, 61
Davies, Thomas, 87
Deere
    Kitty, 104, 110, 111
    Matthew, 104, 107, 108
Dettingen (Battle of), 26
Devon, 17, 22, 63
Dictionary of Welsh Biography, 43
Dowlais, 22
Dundas, Henry, 78

E
East India Company, 43
Edmondes
    John, 116
Edward (Black Prince), 19
Edward IV, 31
Edwin
    Charles, 44, 56, 64, *See* Wyndham: Charles
    Lady Catherine, 44-46

Lady Charlotte, 44, 46, 85, 87
Samuel, 44, 46-47
Sir Humphrey, 43, 44
Evans, Thomas Christopher. *See* Cadrawd

F
Finglas, 25, 27
Fitzhamon, Robert, 17-18, 23, 55, 63, 108
Fleet Prison, 90
Flemingston, 45-46, 69
Flower
Elizabeth, 27
Henry, 25-26
Mary. *See* Nicholl:Mary (Remenham)
William (2nd Viscount), 67
William (3rd Viscount), 67
Fonmon Castle, 43, 52
Fox, Charles James, 77

G
Gam, Dafydd, 55
Gentry, 10-13, 20-24, 29, 35-38, 40, 47, 50, 54-56, 61, 70, 72-74, 76, 81, 84, 88, 106-111, 118-120, 122, 124-129
Definition, 12
George II, 26, 46
George III, 9, 40, 46, 77
Georgiana, Duchess of Devonshire, 26, 84, 86, 92-93
Glamorgan, 9-11, 13-19, 21-24, 29-34, 36, 38, 40, 43-47, 49-50, 55-56, 59, 62-63, 72-73, 77, 81, 85, 88-89, 93, 95, 100, 104-105, 107-109, 114-116, 118, 121, 124, 126-129
Gloucester, 16, 18, 22, 49
Godwin, William, 86
Gorsedd of the Bards of the Island of Britain, 11
Gower, 24

Great Sessions, 20, 106

H
habeas corpus, 78
Halswell, 67, 68, 70, 76
Ham Manor. *See* The Ham
Hamilton
    Lady Charlotte. *See* Edwin: Lady Charlotte
    Lady Mary, 85
Harris
    Howell, 87
    Thomas, 87
Hastings, Selina, Countess of Huntingdon, 87
Hearth Tax returns for Glamorgan, 36
Henry VI, 31
Henry VII, 32, 49
Henry VIII, 19, 38, 105
Hoare, Joseph, 96–98, 101

J
Jacobins, 28
Jenkins, Leoline, 96–98
Johnson, Joseph (publisher), 100
Jones, Daniel, 115, 117–118
Jones, Reverend John, 67
Jones, Robert, 43, 52, 115
Justices of the Peace, 20, 38, 105

K
Kemeys
    Sir Charles, 81
Kemys
    Lady Jane. *See* Tynte, Lady Jane

Kemys-Tynte, Charles, 81, 88
King, Peter, Baron & Lord Chancellor, 50

L
Laws of Hywel Dda, 18, 20
Libby, Ellen Webber, 121
Llancarfan, 69, 126
Llandaff, 30-32, 34-36, 55-56, 98, 101
Llandough, 97-98, 100, 126
Llanmaes, 59, 62, 68-69, 71-72
Llanmihangel, 42-45, 47, 64, 85, 87, 125, 127
Llantwit Major, 42, 58, 62-63, 118
Louis XVI, 29, 78

M
Mackworth
    Sir Herbert, 57
    Sir Humphrey, 40, 41, 56
Magna Carta, 49, 117
Malkin
    Benjamin Heath, 95, 99, 101
    Charlotte. *See* Williams, Charlotte
Mansel
    Sir Edward, 35, 40
Mansell
    Sir Edward, 35-37, 40-41, 45, 56, 112-113
    Thomas, Baron, 41, 44
    Margam, 35, 40, 43, 122, 124
Marie Antoinette, 29, 78, 86
Mathew
    Admiral Thomas, 32
    Edmund, 33-34, 115
    Edward, 30-39, 41-42, 44-45, 47, 108, 124, 126
    Sir David, 31

        Sir William, 32-33
        William (Governor), 32
    Mathews
        Humphrey, 36
        Thomas William, 33
    Matthews Family
        Aberaman, 35
        Castell-y-Mynach, 31, 35-37
        Irish peers, 26, 29
        Llandaff, 30
        Pencoed, 33, 36
        Radyr, 30-31, 33-34
    Matthews, Ann (Iolo's Mother), 30, 47, 53, 57, 62-64, 68, 71, 82-84, 89, 94, 105-110, 119-120, 123-125
    Merrick, Rice, 34
    Merthyr Mawr, 71, 73
    Merthyr Tydfil, 22
    Methodism, 45, 87
    Monmouth, 81, 88-89, 91, 93
    Monmouthshire, 20, 62, 81, 89, 104
    More, Hannah, 86
    Morganwg
        Iolo, 10-16, 20-25, 28-30, 32, 34-35, 37, 41-42, 45-50, 52-54, 56-59, 62-64, 66, 68-73, 75-80, 82-84, 86, 89-95, 97-105, 107-108, 110-114, 116-122, 124-129

N
National Library of Wales, 35, 52, 57, 64, 74, 89, 114
Neath, 22, 31, 40, 55
Nichol
    Illtyd (elder), 62-66
Nicholl
    Illtyd (Younger), 68-69, 89
    John (Llanmaes), 68-69, 71-72

John (Remenham), 7, 13, 60-63, 65-67, 69, 70-73, 92, 97, 100, 107, 118

Mary (Remenham), 13, 24-29, 59, 60, 62-68, 70, 75-77, 84, 91

Sir John, MP, 71

Whitlock, 62-66, 68, 71, 84, 106-107, 118, 125

William, of Caerleon, 89

Nicolas, Dafydd, 45, 57, 124

O

Old Windsor, 27, 60, 93

Ormond
(Marquis of), 25

Oudenarde (Battle of), 26

Our Lady of Penrhys, 31

Oxford, 27, 61, 66-67, 69, 70, 96-99

Oxford University

Bodleian Library, 97

Jesus College, 61, 64, 96-98, 101

P

Pentyrch, 33

Perdita. *See* Robinson, Mary

Petit, Catherine. *See* Seys, Catherine

Pitt the Younger, William, 78

Poems, Lyrical and Pastoral, 13, 27-28, 30, 57, 69, 91, 99, 120

Pontneddfychan, 54

Pontypool, 22

Price, Elizabeth. *See* Seys: Elizabeth

Prince of Wales, 9-11, 13, 28, 46, 75-79, 84, 91, 93, 95, 102-103, 123, 125, 127-128

Princess Augusta of Saxe-Coburg, Dowager Princess, 46

R

Radyr, 30-31, 33-34
Rees
    William (Iolo's solicitor), 112
Remenham, 13, 24-25, 59-67, 69-71, 84, 91, 98-99, 107, 118
Ridge
    Elizabeth, 27
Ridge, William, 67
Roberts
    Margaret (Peggy), 104, 111, 113, 122
Rees, 56-57, 111-113
Robinson
    Maria Elizabeth, 88
    Mary, 79, 82-93, 95, 103, 120, 124
    Thomas, 87, 90

S

Seys
    Ann (Lady King), 48, 50, 58, 79, 82-83
    Catherine, 82-84
    Elizabeth, 52, 58, 69, 84
    Evan, 64
    Evan (husband of Elizabeth), 84
    Richard (I), 47, 49-50
    Richard (II), 50-51
    Richard (III), 50-51, 82-84
    Richard (IV), 51-52, 54
    Roger (disinherited), 49-50, 82-83
    Wenllian, 51-55, 57-58, 68, 84, 119
Sheridan, Richard Brinsley Butler, 77
Sheriff
    Glamorgan, 44

Monmouthshire, 89, 104
of Glamorgan, 32-33, 43-44, 63, 104-105, 107, 115
Skenfrith, 30
Slave trade, 22
Somerset, 17, 21-22, 63, 80-81, 84, 88-89, 121
Statutum Walliae, 105
Swansea, 22

T
Talbot, Thomas Mansel, 112
Talgarth, 87, 93
Talygarn, 56, 98
Taxes, Assessment of, 38
The Ham, 62-65, 69, 70-71, 89, 118, 127
Thomas
    Sir Robert, 43
Tir Iarll, 18, 21, 46, 73, 114
Tower Colliery, 15
Traherne
    Llywellyn, 115-116, 127
    Reverend John Montgomery, 117
Trefeca (Trevecca), 87-88
Tregunter, 87
Tudor, Jasper, 19, 49
Turbervilles, 18, 31, 63
Ty'n Caeau, 30, 34
Tynte
    Lady Jane, 89

V
Vale of Glamorgan, 73
Varinton, Elizabeth née Petit, 89

W

Walters
    Reverend Daniel, 97
    Reverend John, the elder, 97
    Reverend John, the younger, 97
War of the Spanish Succession, 37
Waring, Elijah, 54, 78, 108
Wesley, John, 87
Wilkes, John, 78
William III, 40, 43
William IV, 28
William of Orange. *See* William III
Williams
    Charlotte, 95, 97, 99
    Edward. *See* Morganwg:Iolo
    Elizabeth, 101, 119
    John, 121
    Miles, 121
    Reverend Thomas, 95
    Taliesin, 64, 117
    Thomas, 95, 97–98
Wollstonecraft, Mary, 86
Wyndham
    Caroline, Countess of Dunraven and Mount-Earl, 77
    Charles, 45, 47
    Thomas, 56, 77, 125
Wyndham Grenville, William, 78

Y

Young
    Arthur, 22
    Ystradowen, 104

Author Profile

Emlyn Phillips is a native of the Vale of Glamorgan, and grew up in the same streets and lanes that Iolo knew. A second-language Welsh-speaker, he is a qualified coach and hypnotherapist, having previously been a lecturer at universities and polytechnics in Wales, China and Singapore. He has also worked in Wales' twin country of Lesotho, and in Russia. He has a BA (Hons) in International Relations, an MSc in Computer Science, and an MBA. He was named "Best New Writer of 2022" by Planet: The Welsh Internationalist.

***

What Did You Think of *A Gentleman of Glamorgan: Iolo Morganwg, the Prince of Wales, and the Gentry of Glamorgan?*

A big thank you for purchasing this book. It means a lot that you chose this book specifically from such a wide range on offer. I do hope you enjoyed it.

Book reviews are incredibly important for an author. All feedback helps them improve their writing for future projects and for developing this edition. If you are able to spare a few minutes to post a review on Amazon, that would be much appreciated.

Publisher Information

Rowanvale Books provides publishing services to independent authors, writers and poets all over the globe. We deliver a personal, honest and efficient service that allows authors to see their work published, while remaining in control of the process and retaining their creativity. By making publishing services available to authors in a cost-effective and ethical way, we at Rowanvale Books hope to ensure that the local, national and international community benefits from a steady stream of good quality literature.

For more information about us, our authors or our publications, please get in touch.

www.rowanvalebooks.com
info@rowanvalebooks.com

Printed in Great Britain
by Amazon

41943266R00093